P9-BYN-223

Fodor's
25 Best

BARCELONA

How to Use This Book

KEY TO SYMBOLS	
✚ Map reference to the accompanying fold-out map	🚢 Nearest riverboat or ferry stop
✉ Address	♿ Facilities for visitors with disabilities
☎ Telephone number	❓ Other practical information
🕐 Opening/closing times	▷ Further information
🍴 Restaurant or café	ℹ Tourist information
🚃 Nearest rail station	✋ Admission charges: Expensive (over €10), Moderate (€6–€10), and Inexpensive (€5 or less)
Ⓜ Nearest metro (subway) station	
🚌 Nearest bus and/or tram route	

This guide is divided into four sections

● Essential Barcelona: An introduction to the city and tips on making the most of your stay.

● Barcelona by Area: We've broken the city into five areas, and recommended the best sights, shops, entertainment venues, nightlife and restaurants in each one. Suggested walks help you to explore on foot.

● Where to Stay: The best hotels, whether you're looking for luxury, budget or something in between.

● Need to Know: The info you need to make your trip run smoothly, including getting about by public transport, weather tips, emergency phone numbers and useful websites.

Navigation In the Barcelona by Area chapter, we've given each area its own colour, which is also used on the locator maps throughout the book and the map on the inside front cover.

Maps The fold-out map with this book is a comprehensive street plan of Barcelona. The grid on this fold-out map is the same as the grid on the locator maps within the book. We've given grid references within the book for each sight and listing.

Contents

CONTENTS

Introducing Barcelona

Self-confident, prosperous and buzzing Barcelona, capital of the autonomous Spanish region of Catalonia, is one of Europe's most compelling cities, pulling in millions of annual visitors who flock here to experience its style and diversity.

So, what's it got? The answer is something for everyone: stunning architecture, fine museums, excellent shopping, some inspirational food, and great cafés and nightlife. Not to mention the bonus of the city's seafront position, its medieval core, spacious boulevards and surrounding green hills.

The last decades have seen huge social and economic advances, bringing vast building projects, such as the extension of the metro line to the airport, that have changed the face of the city. Tourism remains fundamental to the economy, but Barcelonins complain about its impact on rents and the changing fabric of the neighbourhoods. Ada Colau, a former street activist who was elected mayor in 2015, has tried to curb property speculation and encourage local businesses.

Catalonia, with 16 per cent of Spain's population, creates over 20 per cent of the country's GDP. Like the rest of Spain, it was hard hit by the global economic crisis of 2008, which fuelled the Catalan independence movement. With a pro-independence coalition in power, a referendum on independence went ahead on 1 October 2017, despite being ruled illegal by the Spanish constitutional court. The Spanish government took control of Catalonia and called new elections for 21 December, which were narrowly won by pro-independence parties. The coming years will require considerable negotiating skills and compromises; fortunately the Catalans have always been skilled at this and their outward-looking and tolerant character will continue to attract visitors from around the world.

FACTS AND FIGURES

- Population: 1,608,746
- Area: City 101.4sq. km (39sq. miles)
- Highest point in Barcelona: Tibidabo (542m/1,777ft)
- The Port of Barcelona welcomed more than 2.6 million passengers in 2016
- More than 8.3 million tourists visited the city in 2016
- Most spoken language: Spanish, followed by Catalan

CONSTITUTIONAL CRISIS

When Catalonia held its referendum on independence in 2017, turnout was less than 50 per cent, but 90 per cent of the votes were in favour of secession so independence was declared. The Spanish government responded by taking control of the region, imprisoning politicians responsible for the referendum and calling new elections—which, however, were also won by pro-independence parties.

CATALAN CHEFS

Catalonia's restaurants have earned more Michelin stars than anywhere else in Spain. Its famous chefs include Ferran Adrià, who brought deconstructivist gastronomy to dazzling new heights with his foams and emulsions at the legendary (sadly now defunct) El Bulli; while his equally daring brother, Albert, is behind a group of spectacular restaurants (such as Tickets) in Barcelona.

CLIMBING THE CASTLE

Seize the chance to catch the *castellers*, clubs of locals who build human castles up to 10 levels during the city's *La Merce* festival (five days around 24 Sep). Participants climb upon each other's shoulders to form 15m-high (50ft) constructions, traditionally topped by a small child, the *anxaneta*. The real heroes are the stalwarts taking the strain at the bottom level of the spectacle.

A Short Stay in Barcelona

DAY 1

Morning Start your day in the **Barri Gòtic** (▷ 49), taking in the **Catedral** (▷ 42–43), the **Plaça de Sant Jaume** (▷ 51) and the **Plaça del Rei** (▷ 51), where, if your imagination is fired by the sense of history, you can learn more at the **Museu d'Història de Barcelona** (▷ 44–45). By 11.30, things are livening up on the **Ramblas** (▷ 46–47), so stroll up and down, pausing for a coffee, to soak up the atmosphere of Barcelona's most iconic thoroughfare. Take in the flower-sellers and street entertainers and then, if you've got the energy, walk along the waterfront beside the **Port Vell** (▷ 68–69) before heading up Via Laietana and turning right into the **Ribera** (▷ 73), one of Barcelona's oldest but coolest areas.

Lunch Enjoy a quintessentially Spanish lunch of freshly prepared tapas at **Senyor Parellada** (▷ 78) on Carrer de l'Argenteria.

Afternoon Head down the street for the Plaça Santa Maria and spend a quiet moment in the beautiful Gothic church of **Santa Maria del Mar** (▷ 70–71) before heading up Carrer Montcada, one of the old city's loveliest streets, to visit the **Museu Picasso** (▷ 64), housed in a series of stunning late medieval merchants' houses.

Dinner Cross the Via Laietana and head through Carrer Jaume I and down Carrer Ferran for a drink at an outdoor table in the elegant **Plaça Reial** (▷ 51) before sampling a real Catalan dinner at **Can Culleretes** (▷ 57–58) just up the street, where classic local cooking has been served since 1786.

Evening Walk north through the old city, or take a taxi, to enjoy a performance in the stunning *modernista* surroundings of the **Palau de la Música Catalana** (▷ 65).

DAY 2

Morning Take the red-route Bus Turístic in the **Plaça de Catalunya** (▷ 50) and sit back for the half-hour or so ride to **Montjuïc** (▷ 30). Alight at the **Museu Nacional d'Art de Catalunya** (▷ 31), pausing on the terrace to take in the city views. Spend a couple of hours in the museum, perhaps concentrating on the superb Romanesque fresco collection. If more culture appeals, hop back on the bus and take in either the **Fundació Joan Miró** (▷ 26–27), on the other side of Montjuïc or the **Museu Marítim** (▷ 24–25), at the foot of the Ramblas, before heading along the waterfront to **Barceloneta** (▷ 62).

Lunch Have lunch with the locals at the **Can Solé** (▷ 77), a great seafood restaurant with a fabulous selection of paellas, fresh fish, lobsters and prawns, before returning to Plaça de Catalunya.

Afternoon Board a red-route bus, which will take you up the Passeig de Gràcia, where you can get off to visit the **Mansana de la Discòrdia** (▷ 84–85), a block containing a trio of compelling *modernista* houses, and then walk north to visit Gaudí's most famous civil building, **La Pedrera** (▷ 88–89). From here, head east to his best-known creation, the **Sagrada Família** (▷ 90–91). By 6, the streets around the Passeig de Gràcia will be bustling, and it's a good time for some serious retail therapy.

Dinner Round off your homage to *modernisme* with a late-ish dinner at **Casa Calvet** (▷ 97), an innovative restaurant housed in a Gaudí-designed building.

Evening You could end the day with a couple of hours' partying at **Luz de Gas** (▷ 96), with its variety of live acts, or simply wind down over a late-night drink at a bar.

Top 25

▶ ▶ ▶

Barceloneta ▷ 62
Densely built 18th-century fishermen's quarter famous for its village ambience.

La Boqueria ▷ 48
Explore the city's celebrated market, packed with fresh goods and exotic produce.

Camp Nou ▷ 104 Visit the famous stadium, home to one of the world's most loved football teams.

Shopping in the Barri Gòtic ▷ 49 Discover the specialist shops, galleries, boutiques and chain stores in this maze of streets in the oldest part of the city.

Santa Maria del Mar ▷ 70–71 Barcelona's most beautiful Gothic church, Our Lady of the Sea, dominates the Born area.

Sagrada Família ▷ 90–91 Gaudí's visionary project, and Barcelona's most famous site, now finally nearing completion.

Las Ramblas ▷ 46–47 Strolling along Barcelona's most famous street is a must-do experience.

Port Vell ▷ 68–69 The Old Port is now a Seafront shopping and entertainment development.

Port Olímpic and the Beaches ▷ 67 Marinas, promenades and sandy beaches draw the crowds.

La Pedrera ▷ 88–89
Gaudí's controversial apartment block is one of the icons of the city.

Park Güell ▷ 86–87
Gaudí's amazing hilltop park is considered one of the city's treasures.

Parc de la Ciutadella ▷ 66 This delightful park, close to the old city, houses a host of attractions.

These pages are a quick guide to the Top 25, which are described in more detail later. Here they are listed alphabetically, and the tinted background shows which area they are in.

Catedral ▷ 42–43 Barcelona's great cathedral is a splendid example of Catalan Gothic architecture.

Drassanes and Museu Marítim ▷ 24–25 Discover the city's maritime past in the royal shipyards.

Fundació Joan Miró ▷ 26–27 Iconic modern museum building that showcases work by Miró.

Gràcia ▷ 83 Discover the narrow atmospheric streets and shady squares of the city's bohemian quarter.

Mansana de la Discòrdia ▷ 84–85 Three famous buildings make up the Block of Discord.

Montjuïc ▷ 30 Green and leafy hill overlooking the port.

Museu d'Art Contemporani ▷ 28–29 Ultra-modern art museum at the heart of El Raval.

Museu d'Història de Barcelona ▷ 44–45 The city's history museum is on the site of the Roman town.

Museu d'Història de Catalunya ▷ 63 This waterfront museum brings the story of Catalonia to life.

Museu Monestir de Pedralbes ▷ 102–103 The monastery is an oasis of calm in a busy city.

Palau de la Música Catalana ▷ 64 Superb concert hall with a full schedule of classical music.

Museu Picasso ▷ 64 Museum in a medieval palace showcasing different periods of the artist's work.

Museu Nacional d'Art de Catalunya ▷ 31 Collections spanning eight centuries of Catalan art.

ESSENTIAL BARCELONA TOP 25

Shopping

Rich and stylish, as attractive to locals and Spaniards from outside Catalonia as it is to foreigners, the city is second only to Madrid as a shopping destination. The contrast between tiny, old-world specialist shops and the glittering bastions of 21st-century retail therapy is striking.

Leather Goods and Souvenirs

Branches of some of Spain and Europe's best-known fashion sources are here, as well as haunts for urban trendies. Added to that, there's a wealth of serious, well-priced leather goods in every style and shade. As for souvenirs of this city of Gaudí, look for useful items with a *modernista* theme—calendars and art books, vibrant ceramics and porcelain. The textiles are inspired; you can pick up gorgeous throws and fabrics in seductive shades and textures from specialist shops and workshops around the city.

Edible Gifts

Gifts you can eat are always popular; the Spanish specialty, *turró* (nougat), almonds and olives spring to mind. Head for the Boqueria market to find items such as strings of dried peppers, aromatic honey, golden threads of saffron, sheets of dried cod, superb hams and cheeses. Spanish nuts and dried fruits are superb, and exciting chocolate boutiques are popping up everywhere.

WHERE TO SHOP

Plaça de Catalunya is the place for department store shopping at El Corte Ingles and El Triangle shopping mall, while the Passeig de Gràcia has the big-name stores and the Eixample has designer labels. You'll find quirky shops in the Raval, Gràcia and El Born in the Ribera, Barcelona's hippest 'hood. The Barri Gòtic is great for crafts and antiques; there is a weekend art and bric-a-brac market held outside the port at the southern tip of Las Ramblas and in front of the cathedral on Thursday. The best flea market is Els Encants at Plaça de la Glories.

Barcelona offers a wealth of fashionable shops, from main street stores to exclusive boutiques

Crafts and Ceramics

Many craft objects can be picked up for a few euros. Basic beige and yellow ceramics from Catalonia's Costa Brava are inexpensive and plentiful. Reproduction *modernista* tiles are a stunning asset to bathrooms and kitchens. The *alpargatara*, the Catalan espadrille (rope sandal), usually has two-tone ribbons that wrap around the ankle, making stylish summer shoes. Most of these can be picked up in souvenir shops, but they are likely to be mass-produced, so try and seek them out in specialist stores.

Specialist Shops

The old city is the home of Barcelona's best specialist shops. Trawling through the narrow streets of the Barri Gòtic and Raval, you'll come across tiny shops devoted to wonderfully esoteric merchandise. There's even a shop devoted entirely to feathers. If you fancy a silk shawl, *mantilla* or intricate fan you'll find it here, as well as deliciously scented candles, flamenco dresses, traditionally made perfumes, soaps and cosmetics.

Designer Bargains

For those who find the temptation of a designer bargain irresistible, there is a cluster of outlets on and round the Carrer Girona, near the Gran Via, where you can pick up fashion at huge discounts. Many of the top mainstream Spanish chains, such as Mango and Nice Things, have outlets here, and there is elegant clothing from Catalan designers Etxart & Panno and Barcelona native Javier Simorra.

There are plenty of gift-buying opportunities in Barcelona—specialist food and craft shops abound

---

THE RAVAL

Along the narrow streets of the Raval, west of Las Ramblas, you will find some of Barcelona's most interesting shops. This is the place to hunt down red-hot design, second-hand fashion, clubwear and dance accessories. Look on and around Carrer Riera Baixa, which is home to a Saturday alternative street market, and the Rambla del Raval, which has a market on weekends.

Shopping by Theme

Whether you're looking for a department store, a quirky boutique or something in between, you'll find it all in Barcelona. On this page shops are listed by theme. For a more detailed write-up, see the individual listings in Barcelona by Area.

Barcelona by Night

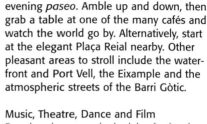

Las Ramblas, the perfect place to stroll, pause and relax, acts like a magnet for an evening *paseo*. Amble up and down, then grab a table at one of the many cafés and watch the world go by. Alternatively, start at the elegant Plaça Reial nearby. Other pleasant areas to stroll include the waterfront and Port Vell, the Eixample and the atmospheric streets of the Barri Gòtic.

Music, Theatre, Dance and Film

Barcelona has a good schedule of cultural eve-ning events. The choice is wide, with everything from opera, orchestral concerts, plays and original language films to jazz, flamenco and Latin American music. You can get information in the entertainment guide *Time Out* (in Catalan weekly, or in English four times a year) or *Que Fem?*, the free listings guide that comes with *La Vanguardia* newspaper every Friday. You can also visit the Virreina Cultural Information Centre on the Rambla (tel 93 316 10 00), or call the 010 information line, where an English-speaking operator will help.

Clubbing the Night Away

Barcelona is a clubber's paradise, with frequent visits from internationally famous DJs, plenty of homegrown talent and a constantly evolving scene. Clubs and bars open and close frequently so pick up flyers and check the listings in *Barcelona Metropolitan* and *Time Out*.

PICK OF THE PANORAMAS

From the slopes of Tibidabo, the huge peak towering behind Barcelona, there are views over the whole city to the sea, which can be appreciated from a number of bars and cafés. The mountain's name comes from the Latin *tibi dabo*—"to thee I give", the words used by the Devil when tempting Christ. Another great view can be had from Montjüic, where there are green spaces to enjoy on summer evenings. Take the *teleféric* up to the castle for a bird's-eye view over the hill and the port below.

Barcelona's diverse nightlife includes some of Europe's top venues, clubs and bars

Where to Eat

Eating out in this city is a pleasure, with the emphasis firmly on seasonal and fresh produce, and a huge range of restaurants, snack bars, tapas bars, cafés and *granjas* feeding residents and visitors day and night.

Breakfast
If you're staying in a hotel, check if breakfast is included in the price. If not, join locals in a bar for a *cafè amb llet* (milky coffee) and croissant or *entrapà* (breadstick stuffed with cheese or ham). Fresh orange juice is available but butter for your toast (*torrada*) isn't—you'll be handed a bottle of olive oil instead. For something more substantial, try a *truita d'ous* (omelette) or *bikini* (toasted ham and cheese sandwich).

Lunch
Lunch is the main meal, and most eat a fixed-price *menu del migdía* in a restaurant. You may get something light such as *escalivada* (roast peppers and aubergine) or a soup for starters, followed by grilled fish or meat or a rice dish (these rarely come with vegetables). Desserts are simple; fresh fruit or yogurt or a *crema catalana* (crème brûlée). A glass of wine or bottled water is included in the price.

Dinner
Dinner is generally a lighter meal and many locals just go for the ubiquitous *pa amb tomàquet* (rustic bread rubbed with tomato pulp) topped with cheese or charcuterie or make a meal out of tapas. Freshly grilled squid, prawns or baked cod are also popular choices.

RESERVATIONS
Booking is advised in mid- to upper-price restaurants, particularly for groups of four or more and on the weekends. For less formal places, such as tapas bars, you can walk in and secure a table, even if you have to wait at the bar for a space to become available. However, if there is an establishment you really want to visit, check out whether booking is necessary.

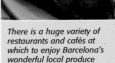

There is a huge variety of restaurants and cafés at which to enjoy Barcelona's wonderful local produce

Where to Eat by Cuisine

There are plenty of places to eat to suit all tastes and budgets in Barcelona. On this page they are listed by cuisine. For a more detailed description of each restaurant, see Barcelona by Area.

Asian
Ikibana (▷ 98)
Koy Shunka (▷ 58)

Cafés
Cacao Sampaka (▷ 97)
Café de l'Opera (▷ 57)

Catalan
Agut (▷ 57)
Café de l'Academia (▷ 57)
Can Culleretes (▷ 57)
Casa Calvet (▷ 97)
Casa Delfín (▷ 77)
Cinc Sentits (▷ 97)
La Cuina del Do (▷ 57)
Embat (▷ 98)
Euskal Etxea (▷ 77)
Els Quatre Gats (▷ 58)
Roca Moo (▷ 98)
Senyor Parellada (▷ 78)
Set Portes (▷ 78)

Italian
Bestial (▷ 77)

Mediterranean
Agua (▷ 77)
Basílico (▷ 38)
Bosco (▷ 57)
Pla (▷ 58)
El Principal (▷ 98)

Mexican
Chido One (▷ 97)

Regional Spanish
El Atril (▷ 77)
El Asador de Burgos (▷ 97)
Mesón David (▷ 38)

Seafood
Botafumeiro (▷ 97)
El Cangrejo Loco (▷ 77)
Can Solé (▷ 77)
Kaiku (▷ 78)
La Paradeta (▷ 78)

Tapas Bars
Bar del Pí (▷ 57)
La Bodega de Palma (▷ 57)
La Bombeta (▷ 77)
Cerveceria Catalana (▷ 97)
Ciudad Condal (▷ 98)
Paco Meralgo (▷ 98)
Quimet & Quimet (▷ 38)
Suculent (▷ 38)
Taller de Tapas (▷ 58)
Tickets Bar (▷ 38)
Vinateria del Call (▷ 58)

Vegetarian
Green Spot (▷ 78)
Teresa Carles (▷ 38)

Top Tips For...

These great suggestions will help you tailor your ideal visit to Barcelona, no matter how you choose to spend your time. Each suggestion has a fuller write-up elsewhere in the book.

A LAZY MORNING
Stroll down Las Ramblas (▷ 46–47) and take in the colourful flower stalls and street entertainment.
Relax over a drink in the faded grandeur of the Plaça Reial (▷ 51).
Amble around the Passeig del Born, the centrepiece of the Ribera neighbourhood, browsing in shop windows and stopping for coffee at a street café (▷ 70).

WATERSIDE LIFE
Head for the Port Vell (▷ 68–69) for craft stalls, walkways and cafés in a glorious seafront setting.
Visit the Aquàrium to discover what's under the sea (▷ 69).

A TOUCH OF RETAIL THERAPY
Stroll the Passeig de Gràcia (▷ panel 94) for credit-card stretching luxury boutiques.
Trawl the narrow streets of the Barri Gòtic (▷ 49), the Raval (▷ 35) and the Ribera (▷ 73) for some of the city's most original stores.
Hit the Boqueria market on the Ramblas (▷ 48) for a spread of food stalls that's among the best in the Med.

VISITING THE CULTURE TRAIL
Trace the artistic development of one of the world's foremost 20th-century creators at the Museu Picasso (▷ 64).
Explore the Barri Gòtic (▷ 52) with its ancient cathedral and museums.
Let the vibrant pictures and sculptures in the Fundació Joan Miró fill you in on the spirit of Barcelona (▷ 26–27).

Clockwise from top left: Mercat de la Boqueria; a cablecar view of the port; Woman and Bird sculpture

MOVING WITH STYLE

For a taste of the past, take a horse-drawn carriage around the Ramblas and waterfront.
Take a harbour cruise on one of the charmingly old-fashioned double-decker *golondrinas* (swallowboats; ▷ 69).
Hire a bicycle from any one of the dozens of outlets or at the tourist offices.

CITY PANORAMAS

Take the elevator to the cathedral roof for a bird's-eye view of the Barri Gòtic (▷ 42–43).
See all Barcelona spread at your feet from the top of the Torre de Collserola on Tibidabo (▷ 106).
For ever-changing city views, stroll through the landscaped greenery of Montjuïc (▷ 30).
Soar high above the port area by the cablecar that runs from Barceloneta to Montjuïc (▷ 30).

ROMANTIC RESTAURANTS

Enjoy the best of Catalan traditional cuisine in the 18th-century surroundings of Can Culleretes (▷ 57), where a series of rambling rooms is decorated with oil paintings and signed photos.
Relax under a parasol on the decking of Bestial and watch the sea while you eat great Italian food (▷ 77).
Soak up the atmosphere while you enjoy old-fashioned service and surroundings par excellence at the Set Portes (▷ 78).
Spend an evening dining in a Gaudí building at the Casa Calvet (▷ 97).

DINING BY THE SEA

Sink into one of the plush sofas right on the beachfront, at stylish Agua (▷ 77) and tuck into fresh seafood and Mediterranean dishes.
Go for unusual paella at Kaiku (▷ 78), made with smoked rice, vegetables from their own garden and seafood straight from the harbour.
You can't get much closer to the sea than at El Cangrejo Loco (▷ 77), which sits right in the middle of the Port Olímpic.

'n Parc Miro; Bestial restaurant by night; flower stalls on the Ramblas; butcher's shop in the Ribera

MODERNISME

See it in all its variations by taking in the Mansana de la Discòrdia on Passeig de Gràcia—three different houses by the biggest names in *modernista* architecture (▷ 84–85).

Relax in a sumptuous interior at the Palau de la Música Catalana (▷ 65), where *modernista* decorative arts and music come together.

Take in *modernisme*'s most iconic emblem, Gaudí's Sagrada Família (▷ 90–91).

FRESH AIR AND GREEN SPACES

Combine fresh air and green space with *modernista* buildings and mosaics in the Park Güell (▷ 86–87).

Stroll past the lily ponds and lake in the flower-filled Jardins Mossen Costa i Llobrera (▷ 30).

Let the kids run wild on the zipline, climbing frames and musical instruments in the shady Parc Joan Brossa (▷ 30).

Bring a picnic and watch the urban spectacle of musicians, giant bubble-blowers and dog-walkers in the Parc de la Ciutadella (▷ 66).

SOMETHING FOR NOTHING

Entertainment in the shape of street performers is free to everyone along Las Ramblas (▷ 46–47).

Sunbathing and swimming on Barcelona's beaches is a great way to have a free day out (▷ 67).

Take advantage of free Sunday afternoon entry in some of Barcelona's top museums, including the Museu Picasso (▷ 64) and Museu Marítim (▷ 24–25).

ENTERTAINING YOUR KIDS

Kids can let off steam on bikes and skates or visit the Zoo Barcelona in the Parc de la Ciutadella (▷ 66).

The Aquàrium at the Port Vell are top of the list for many young visitors (▷ 68–69).

Relax on one of the beaches north of Port Olímpic (▷ 67)

From top: Gaudí mosaic in Park Güell; the beach at Barceloneta; Parc de la Ciutadella; the Aquàrium

Barcelona by Area

The hill of Montjuïc combines its role as a recreational area and a cultural stronghold with style, drawing in thousands of visitors. It overlooks the Raval, an increasingly gentrified neighborhood that is home to the Museu d'Art Contemporani.

Montjuïc and Raval

D'ARAGÓ
VILADOMAT
del
Consell
de
Cent
de
Calàbria
la
Diputació
CARRER DE CASANOVA
CARRER DE MUNTANER
CARRER D'ARIBAU
Universitat
de Barcelona
Rocafort
D'URGELL
Villarroel

DE
LES
CORTS
CATALANES
PLAÇA DE LA
UNIVERSITAT
SANT
ANTONI
Urgell
Comte
Borrell
de
de
DEL
CARRER
SANT
ANTONI
PLAÇA DE LA
UNIVERSITAT
Plaça
Goya
Plaça
de
Castella
de
de
Sepúlveda
Carrer
Valldoncella
DE
Floridablanca
Carrer
Costa
Joaquim
Centre de Cultura
Contemporània
de Barcelona
de
Comte
RONDA
Tamarit
C de Tigre
Carrer de la
Paloma
Museu d'Art
Contemporani
Sant
Antoni
Manso
C de la Riera
Fomen de les
Arts Decoratives
Carrer
Carrer
de
Carrer
de
PAU
Carrer
del Peu de la Creu
Carrer
Alta
de Vidre
Parlament
EL
RAVAL
CARRER
DEL
CARME
C del Marquès
de Campo Sagrado
SANT
Carrer de les Carretes
CARRER
DE L'HOSPITAL
Antic
Hospital
Santa Creu
Santa
Madrona
AVINGUDA
Carrer
Aldana
DE
Carrer
C l'Aurora
C de St
Rafael
d'Elkano
Carrer de Tapioles
Carrer Margarit
RONDA
Carrer de la Riera
Rambla del Raval
Carrer Robador
Carrer de Com
Junta de Com
Carrer Poeta Cabanyes
Carrer Salvà
POBLE
SEC
DEL
Sant
Magalhaes
Carrer del Roser
Carrer
Carrer
Rambla
Sant Pau
del Camp
C del Marquès de
Barberà
Carrer Nou de la Rambla
Carrer
Nou
de la
Paral·lel
Passeig
de Miramar
Passeig
de Lafont
de Cabanes
de
PARAL·LEL
C de Ton
C d'Arc del
Avinguda
C del Cid
Teatre
C Guàrdia
C Morts
MIRAMAR
Plaça
Carles
Ibañez
Carrer
Vila
Carrer Puig ix
Carrer Palaudàries
de les Drassanes
Drassanes &
Museu Marítim
Montjuïc
Miramar
PASSEIG
DE
JOSEP
PLAÇA DE LES
DRASSANES
CARNER
Jardins de
Miramar
Jardins del
Josep Costa
i Llobera
Transbordador
LITORAL
ESTACIÓ
MARÍTIMA
RONDA

E   F   G

Drassanes and Museu Marítim

HIGHLIGHTS

● Medieval navigation charts
● Displays on 19th-century submarine *Ictíneo*
● Figurehead collection
● Fishing caravel of 1907

TIP

● Come in the afternoon to avoid the school parties.

Cut off from today's port by cobbled docksides, the Gothic buildings of the Royal Shipyards are an evocative reminder of Barcelona's long-standing affair with the sea.

Cathedral of the sea By the 13th century, Catalan sea power extended over much of the western Mediterranean. Ships were built in the covered Royal Shipyards, or Drassanes, a series of parallel halls with roofs supported on high arches. The effect is of sheer grandeur—of a cathedral rather than a functional workspace.

Ships on show The Drassanes are now a fascinating museum, displaying paintings, charts, model ships, a number of boats as well as maritime memorabilia. These are all

The Galera Real *is one of the finest boats on display in the museum (left and right), and includes some superbly detailed artwork (bottom right)*

upstaged, however, by the *Galera Real*, a full-size reproduction of the galley from which Don Juan d'Austria oversaw the defeat of the Turkish navy at the Battle of Lepanto in 1571. Built to commemorate the 400th anniversary of the battle, this elegant vessel is nearly 20m (65ft) long. The original was propelled to victory at high speed by chained galley slaves. You can see statues of some of them, along with the commander who stands in the ornate stern, from a high catwalk.

The Santa Eulàlia Admission tickets include a visit to the *Santa Eulàlia*, an early 20th-century three-mast schooner, which is moored a few minutes' walk away. You can explore the ship, and during the summer, it also offers excursions out on the water.

THE BASICS

mmb.cat

➕ F8

✉ Avinguda de les Drassanes s/n

☎ 93 342 99 20

🕐 Daily 10–8. *Santa Eulàlia*: Apr–Oct Tue–Sun 10–8.30; Nov–Feb Tue–Sun 10–5.30

🚇 Drassanes

🚌 14, 36, 38, 57, 59, 64, 91

♿ Few

🎫 Moderate; free Sun after 3pm

Fundació Joan Miró

HIGHLIGHTS

● Painting, *The Morning Star*, dedicated to Miró's widow
● *Personage* (1931)
● Surrealist *Man and Woman in front of a pile of excrements* (1935)
● Barcelona Series (1939–44) Civil War graphics
● Anthropomorphic sculptures on roof terrace
● *Tapis de la Fundació* tapestry (1979)

TIP

● To avoid long walks or lengthy waits for local buses, use the Bus Turístic to access Montjuïc.

Poised on the flank of Montjuïc is this white-walled temple to the art of Joan Miró; its calm interior spaces, patios and terraces are an ideal setting for the works of this most Catalan of all artists.

Miró and Barcelona Born in Barcelona in 1893, Joan Miró never lost his feeling for the city and the surrounding countryside, though he spent much of the 1920s and 1930s in Paris and Mallorca. His paintings and sculptures, with their intense primary colours and swelling, dancing and wriggling forms, are instantly recognizable, but he gained renown for his expressive ceramics and graphic drawings inspired by political turmoil in Spain. Miró's distinctive influence is visible in graphic work all over Barcelona, and locals as well as tourists

Alexander Calder's Quatre Ailes (Four Wings) *(1972) in the grounds of the Fundació Joan Miró (left); 10,000 of Miró's works are on display, including this vibrant woven tapestry (right)*

flock to the Foundation, which is also a cultural hub dedicated to the promotion of contemporary art. Miró's works (11,000 in all, including 240 paintings) are complemented by those of his contemporaries, including Balthus, Calder, Duchamp, Ernst, Léger, Matisse and Moore.

Mediterranean masterpiece The monumental yet intimate Foundation was built in 1974 by Miró's friend and collaborator, the architect Josep-Luis Sert, in a style that remains modern, yet traditionally Mediterranean in its use of forms such as domes, arches, and roof and terracotta floor tiles. It sits easily in the landscape, and its interpenetrating spaces incorporate old trees like the ancient olive in one of the courtyards. There are glorious views over the city, especially from the roof terrace.

THE BASICS

fmirobcn.org

✚ D8

✉ Parc de Montjuïc

☎ 93 443 94 70

🕐 Tue–Wed, Fri–Sat 10–8 (Oct–Mar till 6), Thu 10–9, Sun 10–3

🍴 Café-restaurant

Ⓜ Espanya

🚌 50, 150

🚡 Montjuïc funicular from Paral·lel Metro

♿ Good

💰 Expensive; Articket pass valid (▷ 121)

❓ Book and gift shop

Museu d'Art Contemporani

HIGHLIGHTS

Works in the collection (not necessarily on show) by
● Miquel Barceló
● Jean-Michel Basquiat
● Joseph Beuys
● Antoni Clavé
● Xavier Grau
● Richard Long
● Robert Rauschenberg
● Antoni Tàpies

TIP

● The excellent bookshop has a wide and varied selection, including exhibition catalogues from past shows, designer classics and accessories.

An ultra-modern, gleaming white building by Richard Meier houses MACBA, Barcelona's dazzling contemporary art museum, which spearheaded the Raval neighbourhood's regeneration.

A modern museum For many years Barcelona felt the lack of an adequate establishment devoted to the contemporary visual arts. During the repressive Franco years, its progressive artists enjoyed little official encouragement. Now two major institutions are bringing it back into the mainstream. By any reckoning, the Museum of Contemporary Art, designed by American architect Richard Meier and opened in 1995, is remarkable, its long white walls and huge size a striking contrast to the more traditional buildings across the wide modern *plaça*; the smooth

The spectacular Richard Meier-designed Museu d'Art Contemporani de Barcelona was opened in 1995

granite ledges on the south side are popular with skateboarders. Its exhibition spaces lead to a great atrium and are reached by a spectacular series of ramps and glass-floored galleries, almost upstaging the works on display. Temporary exhibitions featuring local and international artists complement the museum's own collection, which is exhibited in rotation.

Centre de Cultura Contemporània Housed adjacent in the striking old poor house buildings of the Casa de la Caritat, the Centre for Contemporary Culture promotes activities focused on cultural and social themes. Each year sees a season of cultural and theatrical events exploring different aspects of contemporary art and style, from fashion and architecture to modern communications.

THE BASICS

macba.cat

🚩 F7

✉ Museum, Plaça dels Àngels 1; CCCB, Montalegre 5

☎ Museum: 93 412 08 10; CCCB: 93 306 41 00

🕐 MACBA: 25 Sep–23 Jun Mon, Wed–Fri 11–7.30, Sat 10–8, Sun 10–3; 24 Jun–24 Sep Mon, Wed–Fri 11–8 (Thu, Fri until midnight), Sun 10–3. CCCB: Tue–Sun 11–8 (Thu until 10)

🚇 Catalunya, Universitat

🚌 24, 41, 55, 120, H16

♿ Good

💰 Expensive; exhibitions moderate. Articket pass valid (▷ 121)

Montjuïc

TOP 25

The Palau Sant Jordi stadium (left) and the Plaça Sardana (right)

THE BASICS

➕ B8/9, C7/8/9, D7/8/9, E8/9
🍴 Restaurants and cafés
🚇 Espanya, Paral·lel (then funicular)
🚌 61, 50, 55
❓ Telefèric (cablecar) to the upper peaks

HIGHLIGHTS

Buildings and structures
● Fundació Joan Miró (▷ 26–27)
● Magic fountains (Plaça Carlos Buigas)
● The castle for its fabulous views
Gardens
● Parc Joan Brossa
● Mossen Costa i Llobera gardens
● Jardí Botànic
● Teatre Grec amphitheatre

Montjuïc is the green, garden-covered hill that rises imposingly over the port. Crowned by a castle, it boasts two cable-cars, plus gardens and ornate buildings (several now housing top museums) erected for the 1929 Expo.

Gardens and fountains Montjuïc has long provided Barcelona with a green lung. The Jardins Mossen Costa i Llobrera are full of lily ponds and shady corners for picnics, while the nearby Parc Joan Brossa is fantastic for kids, with a zipwire and climbing frames. The Jardi Botànic is superb, and you can also visit the historic botanic gardens, which provide a welcome retreat on summer days. After dark, come for the show at the Font Màgica (▷ 32).

Museums and monuments The Fundació Joan Miró (▷ 26–27) occupies a striking, white *modernista* building set in sculpture-filled gardens. The Palau Nacional (▷ 31) contains the National Museum of Catalan Art, with artworks spanning more than a millennium; like the nearby Poble Espanyol (▷ 34), it was built for the 1929 Expo.

Olympic Ring The 1992 Olympics brought a host of new sports facilities to Montjuïc, including outdoor swimming pools, a new stadium and a beautifully restored historic stadium, all collectively known as Anella Olímpica (Olympic Ring), dominated by Santiago Calatrava's needle-like telecoms tower.

TOP 25

Museu Nacional d'Art de Catalunya

The Palau Nacional dominates the north flank of Montjuïc and houses the National Museum of Catalan Art (MNAC). Its mural paintings, sculptures, woodcarvings and pictures offer a complete overview of a millennium of Catalan art.

Romanesque riches The entire west wing of the ground floor concentrates on the museum's major treasure, the mural paintings rescued from isolated 10th-century churches high in the Pyrenees. This exceptionally rich heritage of Romanesque art was created as Christianity recolonized the mountain valleys during the 12th and 13th centuries. Powerful images of Christ in Majesty, the Virgin Mary and the saints promoted piety among a peasant population following the defeat of the Moors. By the early 20th century, such art enjoyed little prestige and it was only through the heroic efforts of a dedicated band of art historians and archaeologists that so much was saved. There are 21 mural sections, loosely arranged in chronological order.

Medieval to Modernism Elsewhere in the museum, the rooms are given over to a rich collection of Gothic art thanks to two important bequests. The Thyssen-Bornemisza and the Cambó collections include works from El Greco, Tintoretto, Titian and Rubens. Upstairs, MNAC holds a dazzling collection of *modernista* painting, furniture and decorative art, much of it taken from the stately homes of the Eixample and including some fluid furniture from Gaudí.

THE BASICS

museunacional.cat

✚ D7

✉ Palau Nacional, Parc de Montjuïc

☎ 936 22 03 76

🕐 Tue–Sat 10–8 (10–6 Oct–Apr), Sun 10–3

🚇 Espanya

🚌 13, 37, 50, 55, 57 and all buses to Plaça Espanya

♿ Good

💲 Expensive; free 1st Sun of month Articket pass valid (▷ 121)

HIGHLIGHTS

● Aragonese Chapter House Paintings (Room 16)
● The retables by Jaume Huguet (Room 26)
● *Virgin of the Humility* by Fra Angélico (Room 38)
● *San Pedro and San Pablo* by El Greco (Room 33)
● *Ramon Casas and Pere Romeu on a Tandem* by Ramon Casas (Room 54)
● *Granadina* by Hermen Anglada Camarasa (Room 49)

More to See

CAIXAFORUM

fundacio.lacaixa.es

A stunning conversion of a *modernista* textile factory, funded by La Caixa, Catalonia's largest savings bank, this exhibition centre has an auditorium and library as well as impressive exhibition space. In addition to the permanent collection, major international temporary exhibitions are staged throughout the year.

🔲 D7 ⊠ Casaramona, Avinguda del Marquès de Comillas 6–8 ☎ 93 476 86 00 🕐 Daily 10–8 (Sat until 10) 🚇 Espanya 💵 Inexpensive. Some activities free

CASTELL DE MONTJUÏC

The impressive fort-castle facing the sea on Montjuïc has had a dark history since the Spanish government built it in the 17th century to control the rebellious Catalans. Long used as a prison and place of execution, it was here that Lluís Companys, president of Catalonia, was shot in 1940 at the end of the Spanish Civil War. Visitors can find out more about the castle's history in the visitor centre, or simply wander around and enjoy the views.

🔲 D9 ⊠ Carretera de Montjuïc 66 ☎ 93 256 44 45 🕐 Oct–Mar Tue–Sun 10–8; Nov–Feb Tue–Sun 10–6 🚌 Montjuïc Turístic, Telefèric de Montjuïc, PM Bus 💵 Inexpensive. Free Sun after 3pm, all day 1st Sun of month

FONT MÀGICA

Barcelona's "magic fountain" is one of its most pleasing attractions. A relic of the 1929 international exhibition at the base of the stairs to the MNAC (▷ 31), the ornamental fountain looks like any other during the day. But at nightfall it comes to life with a spectacular light-and-music show—the water spurts "dance" to the beats, while a rainbow of tinted lights add a neon glow to the water. Arrive early to get a seat at one of the outdoor cafés or limited public seating.

🔲 D7 ⊠ Plaça Buïgas 1 🕐 Apr–Sep Thu–Sun 9pm–11.30pm; Oct–Mar Fri–Sat 7pm–9pm 🚇 Espanya 💵 Free

Inside the Olympic Stadium (▷ 30); Mies van der Rohe Pavelló statue (right, ▷ 34)

MIES VAN DER ROHE PAVELLÓ D'ALEMANYA

miesbcn.com

Germany's contribution to the Expo of 1929 was this cool construction of steel, glass and marble that reinvented all the rules of architecture and became an icon of modern (as opposed to *modernista*) design. Amazingly, the building was demolished when the fair was over, only to be faithfully rebuilt in the same materials by devoted admirers in the mid-1980s.

➕ C7 ✉ Pavelló Barcelona, Avinguda del Marquès de Comillas ☎ 93 423 40 16 🕐 Mar–Oct daily 10–8; Nov–Feb daily 10–6 Ⓜ Espanya 🤚 Inexpensive

PARC DE JOAN MIRÓ (PARC DE L'ESCORXADOR)

The sculptor's giant polychromatic *Woman and Bird* dominates this park with its orderly rows of palm trees. It is laid out on the site of an old slaughterhouse, l'Escorxador.

➕ D6 ✉ Carrer de Tarragona 🕐 Open access 🍴 Cafés Ⓜ Tarragona, Espanya

POBLE ESPANYOL

poble-espanyol.com

Barcelona's "Spanish Village" provides a whistle-stop tour of the country's architecture and urban scenery. Craft shops, cafés and restaurants and a new museum add to the appeal.

➕ C7 ✉ Avinguda Marquès de Comillas s/n ☎ 93 508 63 00 🕐 Sun 9am–midnight, Mon 9–8, Fri–Sat 9am–4am, Tue–Thu 9am–2am (shops close around 6–8pm; restaurants much later) Ⓜ Espanya 🚌 13, 23, 150 🤚 Expensive

SANT PAU DEL CAMP

This village church nestled in the depths of the countryside when it was built in the 12th century, replacing an older building that was destroyed by Moorish invaders. The highlight is the miniature cloister, flanked by carved columns. The facade's simple sculptural decoration includes the symbols of the Evangelists and the Hand of God.

➕ F8 ✉ Carrer de Sant Pau 101 🕐 Mon–Sun 10–1.30, 4–7.30 Ⓜ Paral.lel

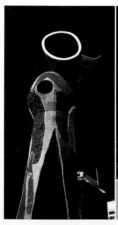

Poble Espanyol

Miró's Woman and Bird *at the Parc de Joan Miró*

A Walk
Through El Raval

On this walk, you can experience the atmosphere of this teeming and historic multi-ethnic working area.

DISTANCE: 2km (1.2 miles) **ALLOW:** 45–50 minutes

START ········

BOQUERIA MARKET
🗝 G7 ▷ 48 🚇 Liceu

1 With the Boqueria on your right walk south for about 50m (55 yards) and take the first right into Carrer de l'Hospital. Walk along here, passing Plaça Sant Agustí on your left, until you come to the Gothic complex of the Antic Hospital on your right.

2 After visiting the inner courtyard, exit and turn right. Continue to the Rambla de Raval, a tree-lined promenade with cafés and an outdoor market on weekends. Turn right. Halfway down on the left is the new cylinder-shaped Barceló Raval hotel and opposite, the *Gat* (cat) sculpture by Colombian Fernando Botero.

3 At the bottom turn right on Carrer de Sant Pau, which crosses the bottom end of the Rambla de Raval. Cross the Rambla and continue along Carrer de Sant Pau to the beautiful church of Sant Pau del Camp.

········ **END**

RONDA DE SANT ANTONI
🗝 F6 🚇 Universitat

8 Continue to the end of Carrer de Joaquin Costa and turn right onto the Ronda de Sant Antoni.

7 Continue uphill over a crossroads and after 200m (220 yards) you will see a pedestrianized street leading to the MACBA (▷ 28–29) on your right.

6 After 50m (55 yards), in a tiny *plaça* with a column topped by a statue of the Virgin, take the left-hand fork. Where the road widens keep the bright facade of the *farmacia* on your left and take the next left turn onto Carrer Joaquin Costa.

5 Take the first left and continue to a T-junction with Carrer de Sant Antoni Abat. Turn right.

4 Leave the church and cross the street diagonally left to take a right turn into Carrer de la Reina Amàlia. Walk all the way along here, passing one crossroads, to the next where you turn right onto Carrer de la Cera.

Shopping

ENTRE LATAS
entrelatas-bcn.com
This stylish little shop specializes in tinned goods, particularly fish and shellfish, which are considered a delicacy in Spain. They come beautifully packaged, which makes them ideal gifts.
E7 ✉ Carrer Parlament 7 ☎ 93 015 47 25 Poble Sec

FLEA MARKET
fleamarketbcn.com
This monthly market takes place behind the Maritime Museum and offers lots of vintage clothing stalls, upcycled gifts and furnishings and street food.
F8 ✉ Plaça Blanquerna Drassanes

NOVEDADES
For a unique gift, take in a photo of a loved one and Lolita's nimble fingers

will make up a cute, cartoon-faced rag doll in their likeness.
F7 ✉ Carrer Peu de la Creu 24 ☎ 93 329 16 36 Sant Antoni, Liceu

OFFBEAT
offbeat.es
This stylish little spot has a wide array of illustrations, paintings, jewellery, fashion and accessories, all produced by local designers and artists.
F7 ✉ Carrer de Sant Vicenç 11 ☎ 93 171 93 03 Sant Antoni

LES TOPETTES
lestopettes.com
Gorgeously packaged soaps, lotions, candles and perfumes are beautifully displayed in this boudoir-style boutique.
F7 ✉ Carrer de Joaquín Costa 33 ☎ 93 500 55 64 Universitat

Entertainment and Nightlife

33/45
facebook.com/33.45bar
Plump yourself down on one of the big leather sofas and watch the world go by at this laid-back bar. A hang-out for local artists, it features changing art exhibitions.
F7 ✉ Carrer Joaquin Costa 4 ☎ 93 187 41 38 Tue–Sun 1pm–2am, Mon 5pm–2am Sant Antoni

BAR ALMIRALL
casaalmirall.com/en/el-bar
This atmospheric *fin de siècle* bar is famous for *absenta*, the supposedly hallucinogenic liquor preferred by 19th-century bohemians, though most locals

settle into the cracked leather sofas with a glass of good whisky.
F7 ✉ Carrer Joaquin Costa 33 Universitat

BAR MAKINAVAJA
Decorated with guitars and comics, this friendly bar hosts rock gigs and serves good tapas.
F8 ✉ Carrer de les Carretes 51 24 hours ☎ 93 441 79 79 Paral.lel

BAR MUY BUENAS
facebook.com/barmuybuenas
The turn-of-the-20th-century Bar Muy Buenas has recently been exquisitely restored and revamped. Its original

Modernista details—swirling woodwork, marble counter—have been preserved, but are now paired with contemporary furnishings to create what has become the neighbourhood's most glamorous spot for tapas and cocktails.

🏠 F7 ✉ Carrer del Carme 63 ☎ 93 807 28 57 🕐 Mon–Thu, Sun 12.30pm–2am, Fri–Sat 12.30pm–3am 🚇 Sant Antoni

BAR ULTRAMARINOS

facebook.com/ultramarinos

Famous for its gin and tonics prepared with a dizzying choice of gins, this friendly little cocktail bar has a relaxed, arty vibe that make it a great place to start the night.

🏠 E8 ✉ Carrer Sant Pau 126 ☎ 65 358 24 24 🕐 Daily 8pm–2am 🚇 Paral·lel

BIG BANG BAR

facebook.com/bigbangbarcelona

This is an atmospheric spot for live music, with everything from jazz and blues to rock and pop, plus perennially popular open mic nights. Entry is free.

🏠 F7 ✉ Carrer d'en Botella 7 ☎ 670 437 709 🕐 Wed–Sun 8.45pm–2.30am 🚇 Sant Antoni

JAZZ SÍ CLUB

tallerdemusics.com/ca/jazzsi-club

This bar belonging to the local music school offers live music nightly. Most gigs start around 7.30 (check the door), with a different genre every night.

🏠 F7 ✉ Carrer Requesens 3–5 ☎ 93 329 00 20 🕐 Closed Mon 🚇 Universitat, Sant Antoni

MARMALADE

marmaladebarcelona.com

Locals and expats head to this cocktail bar-cum-restaurant for pre-club drinks and to relax amid the comfy, art deco furniture and pool table. The bistro-style food is tasty and they serve an all-day Sunday brunch.

🏠 F7 ✉ Carrer de Riera Alta 4–6 ☎ 93 442 39 66 🕐 Mon–Thu 6.30pm–2am, Fri–Sun 10am–2am 🚇 Universitat, Sant Antoni

MAU MAU

maumaunderground.com

This underground club in a back street of Poble Sec is a leading light in the city's counterculture. Listen to live music, view alternative cinema or just mingle at the bar with local bohemians. You may be asked to become a member, though tourists are generally exempt from this.

🏠 E8 ✉ Carrer Fontrodona 33 ☎ 93 441 80 15 🕐 Thu–Sat 9pm–2.30am 🚇 Paral·lel

MERCAT DE LES FLORS

mercatflors.cat/en/

The splendid halls of the old flower market at the foot of Montjüic are now Barcelona's main venue for contemporary dance.

🏠 D7 ✉ Carrer de Lleida 59 ☎ 93 426 18 75 🚇 Espanya

MOOG

masimas.com/moog

Techno goes full blast at one of the city's most popular clubs, which often hosts international guest DJs.

🏠 F/G8 ✉ Carrer de l'Arc del Teatre 3 ☎ 93 301 72 82 🕐 Daily 🚇 Drassanes

TABLAO DE CARMEN

tablaodecarmen.com/en/

This full-blooded flamenco show in Poble Espanyol is popular with locals. You can dine while watching the show, which is staged at least twice nightly.

🏠 C7 ✉ Poble Espanyol ☎ 93 325 68 95 🚇 Espanya 🚌 13, 61

Where to Eat

BASÍLICO (€)

grupandilana.com/es/restaurantes/basilico

This buzzing bistro serves light and lovely Mediterranean-meets-Asian dishes such as goat's cheese salad, fresh pastas and fish tempura in a comfortable, wooden-floored setting.

➕ E7 ✉ Avinguda Paral·lel 142 ☎ 93 423 73 76 🕐 Daily 1–3.45, 8.30–11.30 🚇 Poble Sec

MESÓN DAVID (€)

This wonderfully lively place offers some of the cheapest food in town. Standards are high and the accent is on Galician cuisine, with *caldo gallego* (cabbage broth) and succulent *lechazo* (roast pork) well to the fore. Sample the almond *tarta de Santiago* for dessert.

➕ F7/8 ✉ Carrer de les Carretes 63 ☎ 93 441 59 34 🕐 Daily 1–4, 8–midnight 🚇 Paral·lel

QUIMET & QUIMET (€)

More a *bodega* than a bar, this popular joint has a great selection of wine behind the bar and a fantastic selection of tapas. It's a small place and gets busy, so you may have to eat standing up.

➕ E8 ✉ Carrer del Poeta Cabanyes 25 ☎ 93 442 31 42 🕐 Mon–Fri 12–4, 7–10.30 🚇 Paral·lel

SUCULENT (€€)

suculent.com

A modern take on a traditional taverna, Suculent offers contemporary versions of classic tapas, and particularly pride themselves on their sauces. Star chef Carles Abellán is at the helm.

➕ F8 ✉ Rambla de Raval 43 ☎ 93 443 65 79 🕐 Wed–Sun 1–4, 8–11.30 🚇 Liceu

TERESA CARLES (€€)

teresacarles.com

The fresh and original vegetarian and vegan cuisine at this stylish restaurant is among the best in the city. Chef Teresa's goal is to create healthier versions of the traditional Catalan dishes her mother and grandmother used to make. Wash down your veggie tapas, salad, risotto or pasta with fresh juices with tantalizing names such as "Vegan Vampire".

➕ G7 ✉ Carrer Jovellanos 2 ☎ 93 317 18 29 🕐 Daily 9am–11.30pm 🚇 Catalunya

TICKETS BAR (€€)

ticketsbar.es

Book early for a spot at the city's hottest address: this carnival-themed bar features an exquisite range of gourmet tapas in a relaxed and informal atmosphere. The menu dazzles, with everything from razor clams with lemon "air" to wafer-thin, melt-in-the-mouth ham.

➕ E8 ✉ Avinguda Paral·lel 164 ☎ No phone, reservation by website only 🕐 Tue–Fri 7pm–11.30pm, Sat 1.30–3.30, 7–11.30 🚇 Poble Sec

P AND T

Pa amb tomàquet never fails to comfort a homesick Catalan and no meal is really complete without it. The local version of bread and butter, it consists of a slab of toasted *pa de pagès* (peasant bread) rubbed over with a ripe tomato then drizzled with olive oil and spiked with a touch of garlic.

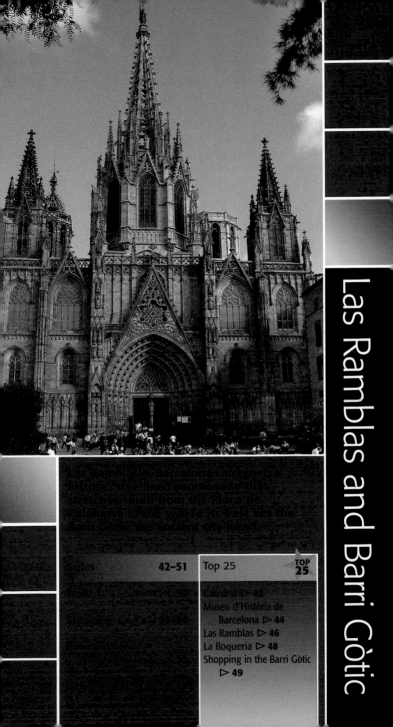

Las Ramblas and Barri Gòtic

Las Ramblas is Barcelona's magnetic, bustling, tree-lined promenade that stretches south from the Plaça de Catalunya to the sea. To its east lies the Barri Gòtic, the ancient city heart.

6

7

8

9

Universitat
de Barcelona

PLAÇA DE LA
UNIVERSITAT

Universitat

RONDA
UNIVERSITAT

CARRER DE BALMES

Carrer

Catalunya

C DE

Casa Municipal
de Misericòrdia

C Elisabets

PELAI

dels

Tallers

C Pintor Fortuny

Las
Ramblas

C Santa

LAS RAMBLAS

Catalunya

CARRER DEL CARME

Palau de la
Virreina

Església
de Betlem

Plaça
Vila de
Madrid

BARRI
GÒTIC

La Boqueria

Plaça
de Pí

CARRER DE
L'HOSPITAL

Liceu

Santa
Maria de Pí

Carrer de Sant Pau

Centre
d'Interpretació
del Call

Gran Teatre
del Liceu

C de Ferran

Carrer Nou
de la Rambla

Palau
Güell

LAS RAMBLAS

Plaça
Reial

C Nou de St Francesc

C de Codols

C de

C de l'Arc del
Teatre

Arts Santa
Mònica

Museu
de Cera

Drassanes

PLAÇA
DEL PORTAL
DE LA PAU

Carrer J A Clavé

Carrer

de

PASSEIG   DE

0   200 m

0   200 yds

F   **G**

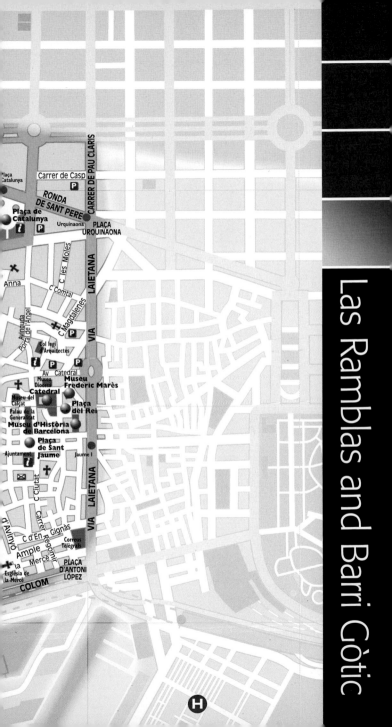

Plaça
Catalunya

Carrer de Casp

P

CARRER DE PAU CLARIS

RONDA
DE SANT PERE

Plaça de
Catalunya

ℹ

P

Urquinaona

PLAÇA
URQUINAONA

VIA LAIETANA

Anna

C de les Moles

C Comtal

Avinguda
Porta de l'Àngel

C Magdalenes

P

Col·legi
d'Arquitectes

ℹ

P

Av Catedral

Museu
Diocesà

Catedral

Museu
Frederic Marès

Museu del
Calçat

Plaça
del Rei

Palau de la
Generalitat

Museu d'Història
de Barcelona

Plaça
de Sant
Jaume

Ajuntament

ℹ

Jaume I

VIA LAIETANA

✉

C Ciutat

C d'Avinyó

Carrer Regomir

C d'En Gignàs

Ample

la Mercè

Correus i
Telègrafs

Església de
la Mercè

PLAÇA
D'ANTONI
LÓPEZ

COLOM

Ⓗ

Las Ramblas and Barri Gòtic

- Crypt with alabaster tomb of St. Eulàlia
- Late medieval and Renaissance choir stalls
- Capella del Santíssim Sagrament
- Cloister

- You won't be able to move around the cathedral during services.
- Make sure your knees and shoulders are covered.

This 14th-century cathedral is one of the finest examples of the Catalan Gothic style, with its soaring spires, cool cloisters and fine array of gargoyles on the roof, which you can reach by elevator.

City church Dedicated to an early Christian virgin and martyr, Eulàlia, the cathedral stands firmly in the middle of city life. Weekends see people gather to dance the elegant *sardana*, a stately Catalan folk dance that symbolizes unity.

Medley of styles The cathedral was begun at the end of the 13th century and was completed, except for the main facade, by the middle of the 15th. However, it was not until the mid-19th century that sufficient funds had been accumulated to construct the facade,

Clockwise from left: the magnificent interior of the Catedral; votive candles at an altar; the imposing Gothic entrance; statues adorning the cathedral exterior; dancers performing the sardana

which was fashionable but somewhat incongruous in its neo-Gothic style. Inside, the cloister is a calm refuge from the city, with magnolias, tall palms, fountain and a gaggle of geese. Of the many side chapels, the most fascinating is the old chapter house to the right of the main entrance; beneath a roof rising 20m (65ft) into a star vault is the Christ of Lepanto, a life-size figure that was carried into the thick of the famous naval battle of Lepanto aboard the royal flagship (▷ 24–25).

The views The elevator on the opposite side to the cloister takes you to the roof from where magnificent panoramic views of the city and the cathedral's spires can be enjoyed from a platform placed over the central nave. The statue on top of the highest spire is of St. Helen.

THE BASICS

catedralbcn.org

🚻 G7

✉ Plaça de la Seu

☎ 93 310 71 95

🕐 Open mornings for worship and prayer only. Tourist visits: Mon–Fri 1–7.15, Sat 12–5.30, Sun 2–5.30. Elevator also open Mon–Sat 10–12

🚇 Jaume I

🚌 45, V15, V17

♿ Good

🎟 Combined ticket: moderate (includes elevator and choir, museum); museum, elevator and choir: inexpensive; church and cloister: free

Museu d'Història de Barcelona

- Roman city streets, shops and workrooms
- Roman mosaics
- Saló del Tinell
- Chapel of St. Agatha: 15th-century altarpiece by Jaume Huguet

TIP

- Entry to the Museu d'Història de Barcelona gives entry to the Museu Monestir de Pedralbes (▷ 102–103) and a clutch of minor sites.

The Barcelona History Museum takes you on a journey through 2,000 years of history, from the ruins of Roman Barcino (now below street level) to the splendid throne room and chapel of the medieval palace that dominates the elegant Plaça del Rei.

Remains of Roman Barcelona The middle of Roman Barcelona extends beneath Plaça de Sant Jaume and Plaça del Rei, while chunks of its walls protrude elsewhere. One of the best-preserved sections faces Plaça Ramon Berenguer el Gran, next to Plaça del Rei.

From Roman times to the Middle Ages The museum on Plaça del Rei occupies a medieval palace moved here in 1931 when the Via

The Casa Padellàs, the medieval palace that houses the Museu d'Història de Barcelona, was moved here stone by stone in 1931

Laietana was driven through the Barri Gòtic. Remains of the old Roman town, including factories and shops, were revealed by excavations carried out during the rebuilding work. Mosaic floors and parts of surrounding walls are among the underground ruins accessible from the museum. Other relics from Barcelona's history include statues and an oil press.

Regal relics Continue your visit above ground in the medieval palace. The highlight is the arched space of the 14th-century Saló del Tinell, the banquet hall where Columbus was received on his return from the New World. Also visit the exquisite Chapel of Santa Agatha, above the Roman wall, which contains a remarkable 15th-century gilded altarpiece by Jaume Huguet.

THE BASICS

ajuntament.barcelona.cat/
museuhistoria

➕ G8

✉ Plaça del Rei

☎ 93 256 21 00

🕐 Tue–Sat 10–7, Sun 10–8

🚇 Jaume I

🚌 45, V15, V17

♿ Poor

✋ Moderate; free Sun 3–8

❓ Souvenir and bookshop (entrance Carrer Llibreteria)

HIGHLIGHTS

- Starting at Plaça de Catalunya
- Flower market
- Baroque Betlem Church
- 18th-century Palau Moja
- 18th-century Palau de la Virreina information area
- La Boqueria covered market (▷ 48)
- Gran Teatre del Liceu
- Mural by Miró on the pavement at the intersection of Carrer Boqueria
- Arts Santa Mònica

Supreme among city strolling spaces, the Ramblas stretches from Plaça de Catalunya to the waterfront. Venerable plane trees frame the broad central walkway, which teems with activity.

Pedestrian paradise Most Catalan towns have their Ramblas, a promenade where people go to see and be seen. None, however, enjoys the worldwide fame of Barcelona's. Sooner rather than later, every visitor joins the crowds along this vibrant central space, where strollers rule and traffic is confined to either side. More than a mere thoroughfare, the Ramblas is a place to linger, to sit, to rendezvous, to watch street entertainers, to buy a paper, to simply breathe in the essence of the city. Until the 18th century, breathing deeply was highly inadvisable;

Clockwise from left: the fountain in Rambla de Canaletes; enjoying the Catalan sunshine; the beautifully decorated Escriba patisserie is a Ramblas institution; a flowerstand on Rambla de Sant Josep

the Ramblas owes its origin to an open sewer along the line of the city walls, which once stood here.

More than one Rambla The Ramblas changes its name several times on its way down toward the Columbus Column, just over 1km (half a mile) from Plaça de Catalunya. First comes Rambla de Canaletes with its famous drinking fountain and newsstands, then Rambla dels Estudis, named for the university once sited here. The Rambla de Sant Josep is also known as Rambla de les Flors, after its profusion of flowerstands. The halfway point is marked by Miró's mosaic in the pavement. The Rambla dels Caputxins with its cafés follows, then the Rambla de Santa Mònica, which retains its earthy charm despite attempts at modernization.

THE BASICS

✚ G7/8

⊙ Catalunya, Liceu, Drassanes

🚌 59, V13

TIPS

● Pickpocketing is rife on the Ramblas, so watch your purse and wallet.
● Bar and restaurant prices are high here and standards low—eat elsewhere.

La Boqueria

La Boqueria is famous for its excellent selection of fresh fish, fruit and vegetables

THE BASICS

boqueria.info
+ G7
☎ 93 412 13 15
🕐 Closed on Sun. Fish section closed on Mon
🚇 Liceu
🚌 14, 59, 91
♿ Good

HIGHLIGHTS

● Breakfast or lunch at one of the traditional counter bars
● Superb selection of fresh fish
● Exotic goodies from around the world

TIPS

● The stalls nearest the front tend to have tourist prices—head to the back for more reasonable prices.
● Come in the morning when the market is in full swing.

Barcelona's central market is a much-loved city landmark. Although the official name is Mercat de Sant Josep, it's better known as La Boqueria. It's a fabulous place to eat, pick up exotic picnic goodies or simply soak up the atmosphere.

Medieval beginnings The market dates back to the 12th century, but it wasn't covered until the 19th century. The elegant *modernista* sign, made of jewel-coloured stained glass, was added in 1912, and the market has been expanded twice since. It is Barcelona's largest and best-known market, famous for its incredible range of produce, which features not only the best Catalan meat, fish, fruit and vegetables, but also goods from around the world.

Stands At the front of the market, nearest the main entrance, you'll find many of the crowd-pleasing fruit and juice stalls, but it's worth plunging deeper to discover some of the most enticing stands. Don't miss the fabulous fish section (closed Mondays), where you can gawp at an eye-popping range of marine life laid out on piles of shaved ice.

Eating and drinking The market is not just a great place to pick up fresh produce; it's also full of wonderful counter bars where you can tuck into a range of cuisines. Most serve traditional Catalan dishes, but you'll also find sushi, veggie options, pizza and more. Prices are similar to a family restaurant, and the food is totally fresh.

Shopping in the Barri Gòtic

Barcelona's Barri Gòtic, the oldest part of the city, is a dense maze of shops, cafés, alleyways and squares. You'll find antiques dealers, galleries and gourmet food stores side by side with quirky boutiques and fast-food outlets.

North of the Plaça del Pí Start at the corner of the Ramblas and the Carrer de la Portaferrissa. Portaferrissa is one of the *barri's* busiest shopping streets, with a wide selection of cheap and cheerful fashion stores. Walk down and take the second right onto Carrer de Petritxol, where clothes shops give way to chic galleries selling antiques and pictures, including landscapes and city scenes of Catalonia and Barcelona. At the end of Petritxol you'll find yourself in picturesque Plaça del Pí. The adjoining Plaça de Sant Josep Oriol has an art market every Saturday and good home decor shops. Several fine shopping streets branch off the square. Take Carrer de la Palla to track down food delicacies and some wonderfully old-fashioned toy stores.

South of the Plaça del Pí Alternatively, take Carrer de l'Ave Maria out of Oriol and turn left onto the top section of Carrer dels Banys Nous. Here you'll find boutiques concentrating on beads and dress jewellery, lovely bags and craft and designer goods. Head south for a splendid old-fashioned hat shop at the junction with Carrer de la Palla and more trinket, jewellery and shoe and ethnic clothing shops along the Carrer Boqueria.

THE BASICS

➕ G7–G8

🚇 Liceu, Catalunya

🚌 45, 59, V13, V15, V17

HIGHLIGHTS

● Browsing at the weekend markets
● An outside table at the Bar del Pí on the Plaça del Pí is the perfect place for people-watching
● Recharge your energy with a sugar fix at any of the *granjas* (cake and coffee shops) along the Carrer Petritxol. Try a *suizo*: a decadent, thick hot chocolate topped with whipped cream

More to See

CENTRE D'INTERPRETACIÓ DEL CALL

This information and exhibition centre aims to explain the history and culture of El Call, Barcelona's medieval Jewish community, which once thrived deep in the Barri Gòtic. They can advise you on where to see its remaining vestiges, including an ancient synagogue, the Sinagoga Major in Carrer Marlet.

🔲 G8 ✉ Placeta de Manuel Ribe s/n ☎ 93 256 21 22 🕓 Wed–Fri 11–2, Sat 11–Sun 11–7 🚇 Liceu 💲 Inexpensive

MUSEU FREDERIC MARÈS

w110.bcn.cat/museufredericmares

There are three main reasons for visiting this museum, named after the sculptor and obsessive collector Frederic Marès: its setting overlooking the courtyard garden of the Royal Palace; its collection of sculpture from pre-Roman times to the 19th century; and the section known as the Colleciò Sentimental, with its surreal array of objects from the 15th to the 19th centuries.

Marès' studio and library have been preserved on the top floors.

🔲 G7 ✉ Plaça Sant Iu 5 ☎ 93 256 35 00 🕓 Tue–Sat 10–7, Sun 11–8 🍴 Café 🚇 Jaume I ♿ Few 💲 Inexpensive. Free 1st Sun of month and Wed and Sun from 3pm

PLAÇA DE CATALUNYA

City life seems to revolve around this spacious central square, not least because of its position at the upper end of the Ramblas. The square was extensively remodelled at the time of the 1929 Expo, when the Metro station was added; now it is the city's principal transportation stop-off. You can catch a bus or train to anywhere in town, including the airport. The largest tourist office in Barcelona is also here. The main landmark is the Corte Inglès department store, and dotted around the square are a number of fountains and statues, including Josep Clarà's *Deessa* (Goddess) and a monument to the popular pre-Civil War politician Francesc Macià.

🔲 G7 🚇 Catalunya

Plaça del Pí

Detail of a mother and child statue in the Museu Frederic Marès

PLAÇA DEL PÍ

Set amid the warren of winding streets between the cathedral and the Ramblas are Plaça del Pí and the adjoining Plaça Sant Josep, two of Barcelona's most beguiling squares. These asymmetrical spaces have leafy shade, laid-back cafés and weekend art exhibitions. A great place to relax, Pí is named for the pine trees that once grew here, as is the serene church, Santa Maria del Pí. The monumentally plain exterior of this Barri Gòtic church conceals an equally austere interior—a single nave in characteristic Catalan Gothic style. The main facade, its statues long since gone, has a fine rose window. The octagonal bell tower is 55m (180ft) high.
➕ G7/8 🕐 Church: daily 9.30–12.30, 5–8 🚇 Liceu

PLAÇA DEL REI

The Plaça del Rei (King's Square) is one of the showpieces of the Gothic quarter, an elegant ensemble of historic buildings that include the medieval royal palace and royal chapel of Santa Àgata (now part of the Museu d'Història de Barcelona ▷ 44–45), the Mirador del Rei Martí, a 15th-century watchtower, and the 16th-century Palau del Lloctinent, which has a pretty garden patio that is open to the public. There's a sculpture by Eduardo Chillida in one corner. The square is also popular with buskers.
➕ G8 🚇 Jaume I

PLAÇA REIAL

With its arcades and classical facades, this grandiose and splendidly symmetrical square is in complete contrast to the crooked streets and alleyways of the surrounding Barri Gòtic. Built in the mid-19th century and modelled on the squares of Paris, it is not very fashionable nowadays, though considerably smarter than it once was. Antoni Gaudí designed the sinuous, wrought-iron lampposts, his first official commission by the city of Barcelona in the 1870s.
➕ G8 🚇 Liceu

PLAÇA DE SANT JAUME

The Plaça de Sant Jaume is named after the medieval church that used to stand here and where the city council used to meet, but its history goes right back to Roman times, when the square was occupied by the Forum and Temple of Augustus. It remains home to the city's most important public institutions: the Ajuntament (City Hall) and the Palau de la Generalitat (home to the Catalan regional government).
➕ G8 🚇 Liceu, Jaume I 🚌 14, 17, 19, 38, 40, 45, 59, 91

The arcaded oasis of the Plaça Reial

The Barri Gòtic

This stroll round the heart of the Barri Gòtic takes you past some of its main sights.

DISTANCE: 1.5km (1 mile)   **ALLOW:** 45–60 minutes

START

PLAÇA DE L'ÀNGEL
G8 Jaume I

END

PLAÇA DE L'ÀNGEL
Jaume I

❶ With your back to the large thoroughfare, Via Laietana, look for the road to your right, Baixada de la Llibreteria. Walk along to the intersection with Carrer de Veguer. Turn right.

❷ Walk to the end to the Plaça del Rei. With your back to the *plaça*, take the right-hand exit onto Baixada de Santa Clara. You then come to the rear of the cathedral (▷ 42).

❸ Turn right along Carrer dels Comtes (the cathedral is on your left). Continue ahead, pass the Museu Frederic Marès (▷ 50) and continue onto the Plaça de la Seu.

❹ Take an immediate left onto Carrer de Santa Llúcia. Turn left onto Carrer de Bisbe and then turn hard right onto the winding Montjuïc del Bisbe to the square of Sant Felip Neri.

❽ Turn right where the road name changes to Carrer de la Dagueria. At the intersection with Carrer de la Jaume I, turn right. The Plaça de l'Àngel, where you started, is on the left. The metro station, Jaume I, is also here.

❼ Continue down Carrer del Regomir then turn left onto Carrer del Correu Vell. In a few steps the street becomes Carrer de Lledó. Continue ahead past Plaça de Sant Just.

❻ Turn left onto Carrer del Call and continue to the immense Plaça de Sant Jaume (▷ 51). Bear right and take Carrer de la Ciutat, which eventually becomes Carrer del Regomir.

❺ Take the farthest exit out of the square onto Carrer de Sant Felip Neri. Turn left onto Carrer de Sant Domenech del Call.

Shopping

ALAMACENES DE PILAR

For combs, shawls, fans, feathers and all Spanish finery, this large shop has the best selection. Items include spotted flamenco dresses and bolts of silk brocade. Prices range from a few euros for a wooden fan, to hundreds for a richly embroidered silk *mantilla* (shawl).

G8 ⊠ Carrer Boqueria 43 ☎ 93 317 79 84 Ⓜ Liceu

ART ESCUDELLERS

artescudellers.com/en/

If it's local ceramics or glassware you are after, this is the place. Wares are laid out by region, from the simple terracotta and green pottery of Catalonia to more intricate, hand-painted tiles and other ceramics from Valencia and Andalucia.

G8 ⊠ Carrer Escudellers 23 ☎ 93 412 68 01 Ⓜ Drassanes

BARRI GÒTIC ANTIQUES MARKET

Bric-a-brac rather than heirloom bargains dominate the stands in front of the cathedral. From late November to late December the market moves to the adjacent Portal de l'Angel and a Christmas market takes its place.

G7 ⊠ Avinguda de la Catedral 6 🕐 Thu 9–8. Closed Jul–Aug Ⓜ Jaume I

CAELUM

caelumbarcelona.com

In convents all over Spain nuns produce delicious cakes and sweets, candles, scented soap and exquisite embroidery. Caelum stocks such delights, beautifully packaged, and there's a café in site too.

G7 ⊠ Carrer de la Palla 8 ☎ 93 302 69 93 Ⓜ Liceu, Jaume I

CERERIA SUBIRÁ

Dating from 1761, this is supposedly the oldest shop in the city. It started as a ladies' outfitters but it now sells candles in all shapes and sizes.

G8 ⊠ Baixada de Llibreteria 7 ☎ 93 315 26 06 Ⓜ Jaume I

EL CORTE INGLÉS

elcorteingles.es

Virtually everything you could ever need sits under the roof of this aircraft-carrier-like establishment. On the several floors between the supermarket in the basement and the restaurant-café at the top are designer fashions, cosmetics, jewels, computers and more. A satellite branch at Portal de l'Angel sells sports clothing/equipment and music.

G7 ⊠ Plaça de Catalunya 14 ☎ 901 122 122 Ⓜ Catalunya

COSES DE CASA

cosesdecasa.com

This fabulous, wood-panelled shop in Plaça Sant Josep Orol specializes in unusual upholstery fabrics, featuring ethnic-inspired prints, weaves and embroidery. Some have been made into take-home goodies such as toiletry bags, cushion covers and gorgeous throws.

G7 ⊠ Plaça Sant Josep Oriol 5 ☎ 93 302 73 28 Ⓜ Liceu

FORMATGERIA LA SEU

formatgerialaseu.com

This shop is dedicated to Spanish and Catalan cheeses. Pop in for a tasting with wine, before stocking up on hard-to-get treats to take home.

G8 ⊠ Carrer de la Daguería 16 ☎ 93 412 65 48 Ⓜ Jaume I

HERBORISTERÍA DEL REI

herboristeriadelrei.com

Since 1860, this well-loved shop has been selling all types of dried herbs, infusions and natural cures, as well as

organic olive oils and cosmetics. The marble fountain in the centre of the shop was once used for preserving leeches.

🟦 G8 ✉ Carrer del Vidre 1 ☎ 93 318 05 12 🚇 Liceu

EL INGENIO

elingenio.cat

Even if you are not in the market for a carnival costume, this shop will delight. El Ingenio is like stepping into a giant dress-up box, with a cornucopia of costumes, masks, wigs and party tricks.

🟦 G8 ✉ Carrer Rauric 6 ☎ 93 317 71 38 🚇 Liceu

KOKUA

kokuabarcelona.com

Manoletes, or ballet pumps, are the only style of shoe stocked here, but they come in myriad leathers, suedes and colours.

🟦 G8 ✉ Carrer Boqueria 30 🚇 Liceu

LA MANUAL ALPARGATERA

lamanualalpargatera.es

This well-established store sells all kinds of rope-soled shoes, some created before your eyes. Their speciality is *espadenyas*, or espadrilles.

🟦 G8 ✉ Carrer d'Avinyó 7 ☎ 93 301 01 72 🚇 Liceu

PAPABUBBLE

papabubble.com

Kids will adore this concept candy store, where you can watch the confectioners roll, twist and form the soft candy into unusual shapes, and then have them personalize it for you. The tastes are as unique as the packaging, and you can try before you buy.

🟦 G8 ✉ Carrer Ample 28 ☎ 93 268 86 25 🚇 Jaume I

PASTISSERIA ESCRIBÁ

escriba.es

Barcelona's finest *chocolateria* is housed in a lovely *modernista* building right on the Ramblas. Stop here to admire the extravagant chocolate creations.

🟦 G8 ✉ Las Ramblas 83 ☎ 93 301 60 27 🚇 Liceu

SOMBRERIA MIL

sombreriamil.com

This century-old shop retains much of its original charm, and offers a wide range of elegant headwear, from the Catalan beret to panamas.

🟦 G7 ✉ Carrer de Fontanella 20 ☎ 93 301 84 91 🚇 Urquinaona

EL TRIANGLE

eltriangle.es

This complex contains, among other shops, FNAC and Camper. FNAC is one of the city's best sources for books and music and it also sells concert tickets.

🟦 G7 ✉ Plaça de Catalunya 4 ☎ 93 318 01 08 🚇 Catalunya

VAHO GALLERY

vaho.es

Vaho were the pioneers in making bags out of recycled PVC banners, and they make unique and practical souvenirs.

🟦 G7 ✉ Plaça Sant Josep Oriol 3 ☎ 93 412 78 94 🚇 Liceu

PICNIC FOODS

Look out for the offerings from the *forn de pa* (bakery) and the *xarcuteria* (delicatessen or charcuterie), great for accompanying slicings from a good *jamón serrano* (drycured ham). Look for *fuet* (a hard Catalan sausage), *chorizo*, *sabrasada* (a Mallorcan paste of pork and paprika) and cured Manchego cheese.

GRAN TEATRE DEL LICEU

liceubarcelona.cat

Destroyed by fire in 1994, Barcelona's Opera House was rebuilt in all its 19th-century glory with added technical advances. It stages ballet and concerts as well as opera.

⊞ G8　✉ Rambla 61–65　☎ 93 485 99 00 (93 485 99 14 to arrange visits)　🚇 Liceu

HARLEM JAZZ CLUB

harlemjazzclub.es

Barcelona's oldest jazz club still packs in the crowds, who come to enjoy some of the most varied music in the city—everything from jazz to flamenco fusion.

⊞ G8　✉ Carrer de la Comtessa de Sobradiel 8　☎ 93 310 07 55　🕐 Closed Sun, 2 weeks in Aug　🚇 Jaume I

JAMBOREE

masimas.com/jamboree

An underground jazz club that's almost cavelike, hosting blues, soul, jazz, funk and occasional hip-hop live bands. On weekends, the dance floor opens at 1am and quickly fills up.

⊞ G8　✉ Plaça Reial 17　☎ 93 319 17 89 🕐 Daily 9pm–5am　🚇 Liceu

KARMA

karmadisco.com

This basement venue is still the most popular of several lively rock clubs around Plaça Reial.

⊞ G9　✉ Plaça Reial 10　☎ 93 302 56 80 🕐 Tue–Sun midnight–5am　🚇 Liceu

LA MACARENA

macarenaclub.com

This tiny techno club in the back streets of the Barri Gòtic pulls in plenty of customers post 2am. International DJs regularly play here, and the minuscule dance floor gets jam packed.

⊞ G8　✉ Carrer Nou de Sant Francesc 5 🕐 Mon–Thu, Sun 11.30–4.30, Fri–Sat 11.30–5.30　🚇 Drassanes

MENAGE À TROIS

menageatrois.es

This intimate little bar is great for a quiet cocktail and bar food, either inside or out, overlooking the Roman remains in Plaça Vila de Madrid.

⊞ G7　✉ Carrer d'en Bot 4　☎ 93 301 55 42 🕐 Closed Mon　🚇 Catalunya

SOR RITA

sorritabar.es

Fabulously kitsch—the ceiling is covered with shoes, and photos of black-and-white cinema idols are mixed in with saints—this bar is a fantastic stop for cocktails.

⊞ G8　✉ Carrer de la Mercè 27　☎ 93 176 62 66　🚇 Jaume I

LOS TARANTOS

masimas.com/en/tarantos

Here you will find some of the best flamenco acts in Catalonia at a conveniently located *tablao* (flamenco club) in Plaça Reial. Performances start at 8.30, and there are several in one evening.

⊞ G8　✉ Plaça Reial 17　☎ 93 319 17 89 🚇 Liceu

NIGHT ZONES

Lively nightlife can be found all over the city. Plaça Reial in the old town is always active, though laws on noise levels have pushed many late-night clubs out into the suburbs, where the action takes place until dawn and beyond. The Eixample area has plenty of classy cocktail bars and summer terraces, while Gràcia, Poble Sec and the new hipster favourite, Sant Antoni, offer a more local, alternative vibe.

PRICES

Prices are approximate, based on a 3-course meal for one person.

€€€ over €50
€€ €25–€50
€ under €25

AGUT (€€)

The Agut family, which has owned the restaurant for the last three generations, has a menu reflecting seasonal availability as well as dishes that are popular all year round, such as *olla barrejada* (a Catalan stew with vegetables and meat) and *fideuà* (fish noodles), cod with red peppers and garlic mayonnaise.

⊞ G8 ✉ Carrer d'en Gignàs 16 ☎ 93 315 17 09 🕐 Tue–Sat 1.30–4, 9–12, Sun 1–4; closed Aug 🚇 Jaume I

BAR DEL PÍ (€)

bardelpi.com

Friendly service makes eating at this tapas bar, delightfully located in the little square dominated by the church of Santa Maria del Pí, a real pleasure.

⊞ G7 ✉ Plaça Sant Josep Oriol ☎ 93 302 21 23 🕐 Daily 9am–11.30pm 🚇 Liceu

LA BODEGA DE PALMA (€)

bodegalapalma.com

This rustic, old-school tapas bar is as popular with locals as with visitors. Get here around 8.30pm to grab one of the tiny marble tables and order a selection of traditional tapas. Service is tourist-friendly without being touristy.

⊞ G8 ✉ Carrer Palma de Sant Just 7 ☎ 93 315 06 56 🕐 Mon–Fri 9am–midnight, Sat noon–midnight 🚇 Jaume I

BOSCO (€)

This charming restaurant behind the cathedral, serves tapas (including their delectable *patatas Bosco*—a variation of the classic *patatas bravas*), as well as more substantial meals. Fresh, modern Mediterranean dishes might include oven-baked turbot, or canelones with wild mushrooms. There's a great-value set lunch menu.

⊞ G8 ✉ Carrer Capellans 9 ☎ 93 412 13 70 🕐 Mon 1–5, Tue–Sat 1–3.30, 8–11.30 🚇 Liceu, Jaume I

CAFÉ DE L'ACADEMIA (€€)

Not really a café at all, this restaurant offers some of the best deals in town on a variety of traditional Mediterranean cuisine. Reserve ahead.

⊞ G8 ✉ Carrer de Lledó 1 ☎ 93 319 82 53 🕐 Mon–Fri 1–3.30, 8–11 🚇 Jaume I

CAFÉ DE L'OPERA (€)

cafeoperabcn.com

Opera-goers and tourists fill the art nouveau interior and terrace tables of this dignified establishment opposite the Liceu. It's a great place for a spot of people-watching on the Ramblas, but that is reflected in the prices.

⊞ G8 ✉ Rambla 74 ☎ 93 317 75 85 🕐 Daily 8.30am–2.30am 🚇 Liceu

CAN CULLERETES (€€)

culleretes.com/en/

Can Culleretes has the distinction of being one of the oldest restaurants in

GALICIAN FLAVOURS

Many restaurants in Barcelona specialize in Galician cuisine. Galicia, the northwest region of Spain, is famous for its seafood—octopus, crab, scallops, clams and sardines are all simply prepared and delicious. Traditional Galician country fare is also excellent; try *empañadas* (pastry filled with seafood or meat).

the city, founded in 1786 as a pastry shop. The menu is like a catalogue of old-fashioned Catalan cuisine, but there are modern dishes, too. Sample the *botifarra* (pork sausage) with beans.

🔾 G8 ✉ Carrer d'en Quintana 5 ☎ 93 317 30 22 🕔 Tue–Sat 1.30–4, 8–10.45, Sun 1.30–4. Closed 1 month in summer 🚇 Liceu

LA CUINA DEL DO (€€€)

Part of one of the city's newest five-star hotels, this elegant restaurant in a stone-vaulted dining room is renowned for its contemporary Catalan cuisine. Choose between the set menus or go à la carte.

🔾 G8 ✉ Plaça Reial 1 ☎ 93 481 36 66 🕔 Tue–Sat 1.30–3.30, 7.30–11 🚇 Liceu

KOY SHUNKA (€€€)

koyshunka.com/KoyShunka/home.html
This is considered one of the best Japanese restaurants in the city, as its clientele of star chefs and local gastronomes confirms. You'll need to reserve, though there are often seats left at the bar, where you'll be entertained by the masterful sushi chefs.

🔾 G8 ✉ Carrer Copons ☎ 93 412 79 39 🕔 Mon–Sat 1.30–3, 8.30–10.30, Sun 1.30–3 🚇 Jaume I

PLA (€€)

restaurantpla.cat
An excellent spot for a romantic candlelit dinner in the Barri Gòtic, Pla specializes in innovative, Mediterranean-based cooking. There's a good choice of vegetarian dishes.

🔾 G8 ✉ Carrer de Bellafila 5 ☎ 93 412 65 52 🕔 Daily 7–11.30pm 🚇 Jaume I

ELS QUATRE GATS (€€)

4gats.com/en/
The Four Cats was frequented by Barcelona's 20th-century bohemian crowd (including a young Picasso). There is a tapas bar up front, while the restaurant is situated in the back.

🔾 G7 ✉ Montsío 3bis ☎ 93 302 41 40 🕔 Daily 9am–midnight 🚇 Urquinaona, Catalunya

TALLER DE TAPAS (€)

tallerdetapas.com
Unashamedly aimed at tourists wanting to try tapas but wary of ordering across the counter, this congenial tapas bar has multilingual menus and plenty of seating—and the tapas are reliably good.

🔾 G7 ✉ Plaça Sant Josep Oriol 9 ☎ 93 301 80 20 🕔 Mon–Sat 8.30am–1am, Sun noon–1am 🚇 Liceu

VINATERIA DEL CALL (€)

lavinateriadelcall.com
This low-ceilinged, Gothic-looking bodega is perceived to be one of the best places to taste *pa amb tomaquèt*, the ubiquitous Catalan "tomato bread" (▷ 38). Try it with all sorts of cheese and charcuterie, accompanied by a glass of rioja from the excellent wine list.

🔾 G8 ✉ Carrer Sant Domenec del Call 9 ☎ 93 302 60 92 🕔 Daily 7.30pm–1am 🚇 Liceu

CATALAN COOKING

Catalonia is generally reckoned to have one of the great regional cuisines of Spain, based on good local ingredients and on seafood from the Mediterranean and the Atlantic. Four principal sauces are used. There is *sofregit* (onion, tomato and garlic cooked in olive oil); with added sweet pepper, aubergine and courgette it becomes *samfaina*. *Picada* is made by pounding nuts, fried bread, parsley, saffron and other ingredients in a mortar. Finally there is garlic mayonnaise, *alioli*.

Port Vell is Barcelona's waterside pleasure zone, with wooden boardwalk, aquarium and leisure complex. Inland lies the historic Ribera, whose two sections, Sant Pere and the Born, are rich in urban pleasures.

5

6

7

8

9

Carrer de Casp

Casa Calvet

CARRER DEL BRUC

CARRER DE GIRONA

CARRER DE BAILEN

PASSEIG DE SANT JOAN

Carrer d'Ausiàs

Carrer

PLAÇA URQUINAONA

RONDA

DE SANT PERE

CARRER

DE TRAFALGAR

Arc de Triomf

Palau de la Música Catalana

Plaça St Pere

CASC ANTIC

Arc del Triomf

Carrer Sant Pere Mitjà

Carrer Sant Pere mes Baix

C. Cortinas

Mercat Santa Caterina

Av F Cambó

C Giralt

C. Portal Nou

PASSEIG

LLUIS COMPANYS

Museu de la Xocolata

Carders

Metges

del

Comerç

Museu de Ciències Naturals

Jaume I

CARRER DE LA PRINCESA

Museu de Cultures del Món

Montcada

Museu Picasso

PASSEIG DE PICASSO

Museu Martorell

Carrer de Comercial

El Born Centre de Cultura i Memòria

VIA LAIETANA

Santa Maria del Mar

Passeig del Born

RIBERA

C. Consolat de Mar

La Llotja

AVINGUDA MARQUÈS DE L'ARGENTERA

Plaça del Palau

DE

ESTACIÓ BARCELONA DE FRANÇA

PLAÇA D'ANTONI LÓPEZ

PG ISABEL II

Plaça de Pau Vila

Barceloneta

CARRER DEL DR AIGUADER

PLAÇA DEL PORTAL DE LA PAU

PASSEIG

DE

COLOM

Monument a Colom

Palau de Mar

RONDA

LITORAL

CARRER DEL DR AIGUADER

PASSEIG

DE

Moll de Bosch i Alsina

Dàrsena Nacional

Moll d'Espanya

Museu d'Història de Catalunya

Carrer de Ginebra

Carrer Balboa

PASSEIG DE JOAN DE BORBÓ

CARRER DE JOAN DE BORBÓ

Plaça de Pompeu Fabra

Parc de la Barceloneta

Rambla de Mar

Reial Club Marítim

Dàrsena del Comerç

Plaça Barceloneta

Plaça de la Font

Moll de la Barceloneta

Port Vell

Aquàrium

BARCELONETA

Carrer Sant Carles

Carrer Almirall Cervera

C d'Andrea Dòria

Plaça Brugada

Poliesportiu Marítim

San Miquel del Port

Passeig

Marítim

0   250 m
0   250 yds

G

H

FLOR

DE

Marc

Nàpols

de

d'Alí

ROGER

Carrer de Ribes

DE

CARRER

CARRER

Sardenya

CARRER DE LA MARINA

CARRER DE LA MARINA

Carrer de Lepant

AVINGUDA

Bel

MERIDIANA

Auditori Municipal y Museo de la Música

Carrer de Tànger

d'Àlaba

Carrer Sancho de Avila

ANTIGA ESTACIÓ DEL NORD

Parc de l'Estació del Nord

Marina

DELS

ALMOGÀVERS

Carrer

CARRER

CARRER DE BUENAVENTURA MUÑOZ

CARRER DE PALLARS

PASSEIG DE PUJADES

MARINA

LA

d'Àustria

Zamora

Carrer de Pujades

Bogatell

D'ALABA

CARRER

Carrer

WELLINGTON

DE

Carrer

Carrer de Llull

de

de

Joan

AV

de Pamplona

D'ÀVILA

Parc de la Ciutadella

Parlament de Catalunya

Universitat Pompeu Fabra

Fargas

Carrer

Carrer

de

DE

Ramon

Turró

Carrer del

Carrer

CARRER

CARRER

Trias

del

Doctor

Trueta

R Sensat

Arquitecte Sert

Bogatell

Zoo Barcelona

DE

Carrer

Carrer

AVINGUDA

D'ICÀRIA

CIRCUMVAL.LACIÓ

Ramon

Ciutadella Vila Olímpica

CARRER

Carrer de

Vila Olímpica

RONDA LITORAL

Plaça Voluntaris Olímpics

Parc del Port Olímpic

Plaça dels Campions

Plaça Dr Pont i F

i da

PG MARÍTIM DEL NOVA ICÀRIA

C

de Barceloneta

jep

Cas

Carrer

Torre Mapfre

Moll de Mestral

Port Olímpic

Moll de Gregal

Moll de Xaloc

J

K

Barceloneta

The popular beach at Barceloneta (left); Frank Gehry's Fish (right)

THE BASICS

* ➕ H9
* ✉ Barceloneta
* 🚇 Barceloneta
* 🚌 39, 45, 59, D20, V15
* ❓ Barceloneta's Festa Major, with music, parades, dancing on the beach and fireworks runs through the 3rd week in Sep

HIGHLIGHTS

* ● Plaça Barceloneta and the baroque church of San Miquel del Port
* ● The Mercat de Barceloneta
* ● Market on Plaça de la Font
* ● Passeig Marítim
* ● The beaches

Barceloneta, with its grid of narrow streets opening onto the beach, was once inhabited by fishermen and dockworkers. It still has a popular, traditional appeal, although there are now more tourists than locals in its tapas bars.

Little Barcelona Displaced by the building of the Ciutadella (▷ 66), many people from the Ribera moved to live in shanty dwellings by the sea. These were swept away and replaced with a planned district of modest homes in the mid-18th century. The narrow streets at its core have survived virtually unchanged, and the fantastic market, now with a striking, contemporary canopy, is still the focal point of the neighbourhood. The Passeig Joan de Borbó, which links the old city with the beaches, is packed with restaurants and cafés, as is the waterfront.

New landmarks The whole of the Port Vell (▷ 68–69) and the beachfront area were entirely redeveloped in the run-up to the 1992 Olympics, when the Hotel Arts and the nearby Mapfre Tower were completed. They remain two of the tallest buildings in the city and, along with Frank Gehry's huge, glistening *Fish* sculpture that sits below the Hotel Arts, are now iconic landmarks. Ricard Bofill's sail-shaped W Hotel closes off one end of the beach. The waterfront area that links it to the Passeig Joan de Borbó has also been completely remodelled, and now boasts a palm-shaded extension to the seafront promenade.

Museu d'Història de Catalunya

Fish restaurants at the Palau de Mar (left); Museu d'Història de Catalunya (right)

Learn about Catalonia's past with a visit to the entertaining Palau de Mar, home to the Museu d'Història de Catalunya. Innovative and interactive exhibits clarify what has gone into the creation of this nation within a nation.

Catalonia! Catalonia! An imposing late 19th-century warehouse Palau de Mar houses this stimulating museum. Although Catalan history may be something of a mystery to casual visitors, it's worth knowing more about—the past speaks volumes about the present and current aspirations. General Franco wanted Catalan identity to disappear altogether; the museum is one of many initiatives that the regional government (the Generalitat) took to restore it. The exhibits have detailed Catalan explanations and simple English ones, and you can book a guided tour in English at the ticket desk.

Intriguing exhibits The waterfront museum highlights themes from history in a series of spaces grouped around a central atrium. There are relatively few objects on display, but exhibits are truly ingenious; you can work an Arab waterwheel, walk over a skeleton in its shallow grave, climb onto a cavalier's charger and test the weight of his armour, enter a medieval forest, enjoy a driver's-eye view from an early tram, and cower in a Civil War air-raid shelter. Sound effects, films and interactive screens enhance the experience, and the temporary shows are of an equally high standard.

THE BASICS

mhcat.net

✚ H9

✉ Plaça de Pau Vila 3

☎ 93 225 47 00

🕐 Tue, Thu–Sat 10–7, Wed 10–8, Sun 10–2.30

🍴 Café

Ⓜ Barceloneta

🚌 39, 45, 59, D20, V15

♿ Good

💰 Inexpensive

HIGHLIGHTS

● Early ship packed with amphorae
● Moorish market stall
● Sinister Civil Guards pursuing insurgents
● Civil War machine-gun emplacement
● Franco-era schoolroom
● 1930s kitchen with objects to handle
● First edition of George Orwell's *Homage to Catalonia*
● 1960s tourist bar with *Speak Inglis/Parle Frances* sign

Museu Picasso

The exterior of the museum (left and middle); a painting from Las Meninas *(right)*

THE BASICS

museupicasso.bcn.cat

⊞ H8

✉ Carrer Montcada 15–23

☎ 93 256 30 00

🕐 Tue–Sun 9–7 (Thu till 9.30)

🍴 Café-restaurant

Ⓜ Jaume I

🚌 45, 120, V15, V17

♿ Good

💲 Expensive; free Sun after 3pm. Articket pass valid (▷ 121)

HIGHLIGHTS

● Ceramics from 1940s and 1950s
● *The Embrace* (1900)
● *Science and Charity* (1897)
● *Gored Horse* (1917)
● *El Loco* (The Madman) (1904)
● *Harlequin* (1917)
● *Las Meninas* suite (1957)
● Cannes paintings of landscapes and doves (late 1950s)

Picasso, Spain's best-known artist, came to live in Barcelona at the age of 14. Many of his formative experiences took place in the old town and a museum devoted to his work is here.

Picasso's palace The Picasso Museum's collection concentrates on certain periods in Picasso's life and artistic evolution, including his time in Barcelona. The work benefits from its magnificent setting: the 13th-century Palau Berenguer d'Aguilar and four adjacent buildings give an excellent idea of the lifestyle enjoyed by the merchant families at the height of medieval Barcelona's prosperity.

At home and away An Andalucian hailing from Málaga, Pablo Ruiz Picasso accompanied his art teacher father and family to Barcelona in 1895. His skills flourished at his father's academy and, later, at art school in Madrid. From 1899, he immersed himself in bohemian Barcelona, frequenting the red-light district on Carrer d'Avinyó, the inspiration for *Demoiselles d'Avignon* (1907). He was a regular customer at Els Quatre Gats (▷ 58), a café whose menu he designed. His first exhibition was held here in 1900, the year he made his first visit to Paris. France was to be his home after that, but he returned to Barcelona many times, and much of the work in his Blue Period (c. 1902–04) was done here. The Civil War, which provoked one of his most passionate paintings, *Guernica* (now in Madrid) put an end to these visits.

The elaborate exterior of the concert hall (left) and the interior (right)

Palau de la Música Catalana

For nearly a century, this glittering jewel has served not only as a concert hall but also as an icon of Catalan cultural life. The profusion of ornament is staggering—a delight in itself.

Catalan icon The sumptuous Palace of Catalan Music was designed by architect Domènech i Montaner as the home of the Catalan national choir, the Orfeó. It was inaugurated in 1908 to unanimous acclaim and became a symbol of the new renaissance in Catalan culture. Montaner gave the building a steel frame to support profuse interior and exterior decoration intended to inspire and instruct. This decoration was the work of his own ceramicists, painters, glassworkers and tilers.

Auditorium Riches cover the main facade, the entrance hall, the foyer and staircase, but the 2,000-seat concert hall is even more ornate. Light pours in through the glass walls and from the roof, from which hangs an extraordinary bowl of stained glass; the curving lines and rich ornamentation give the effect of being inside an enormous Fabergé egg. The proscenium arch is so covered in sculptures it seems to have a life of its own. On the left, a willow tree shelters the great mid-19th-century reviver of Catalan music, Josep Anselm Clavé; on the right, a bust of Beethoven is upstaged by Wagnerian Valkyries rollicking through the clouds. At the back of the stage, the 18 Muses of music emerge from a curving wall.

THE BASICS

palaumusica.cat
➕ H7
✉ Carrer Palau de la Música 4–6
☎ 93 295 72 00
🕐 Guided visits daily 10–3.30; Jul, Aug and Easter Week daily 10–6
🍽 Bar/café
Ⓜ Urquinaona
🚌 17, 19, 40, 45
♿ Good
💰 Expensive (tickets from ticket office in advance)

HIGHLIGHTS

● Catalan singers in mosaic
● Composers' busts
● Proscenium sculpture *Allegory of Catalan Folksong*
● Foyer vaults with floral capitals
● Stained glass inverted dome in the concert hall

TIP

● You have to take a guided tour to see most of the interior, but can visit the foyer café for free.

PORT VELL AND LA RIBERA **TOP 25**

Parc de la Ciutadella

Steps leading to the park (left); the Arc de Triomf (right)

THE BASICS

🔲 H/J8
🚇 Arc de Triomf, Barceloneta
🚌 14, 39, 41, 59

HIGHLIGHTS

● The Cascada
● Castle of three dragons (Zoological Museum)
● *Sorrow* by Josep Llimona
● *Lady with Parasol* by Joan Roig (1884) (in Zoo)
● *Homage to Picasso* by Antoni Tàpies (1983) (on Passeig de Picasso)

In the 1860s and 1870s, the great Citadel, a symbol of Bourbon oppression, was demolished. In its place, the city laid out its first public park, still a shady haven on the edge of the city hub.

The Citadel Covering an area almost as big as the city itself at the time, the Citadel was built to cow the Catalans after their defeat in 1714, by the new Bourbon monarch of Spain, Felipe V. A garrison of 8,000 troops kept the population in check, and the Citadel was loathed as a place where local patriots were executed. In 1868, the Catalan General Juan Prim y Prats came to power and ordered its demolition, a process already begun by the citizens.

The park today The public park that took the Citadel's place shows little trace of the great fortress, though the Arsenal houses the Catalan Parliament. Other structures are leftovers from the Universal Expo of 1888: an ornate Arc de Triomf (Triumphal Arch) and a fairy-tale, *modernista* restaurant designed by Domènech i Montaner and now home to part of the Museum of Natural Sciences. The zoo is to the east (▷ 72), while the geology section of the Natural History Museum is on the southern flank. A boating lake and fine trees and shrubs throughout the park soften the formal layout. The imposing Cascada, an extraordinary fountain incorporating a plethora of allegorical references, was worked on by Gaudí when he was an architecture student.

The marina at Port Olímpic (left); stealing some shade at a café (right)

Port Olímpic and the Beaches

The eye-catching development of the Vila Olímpica, built for the 1992 Olympic Games, is a stunning ensemble of marinas, broad promenades, glittering buildings and open space.

Port Olímpic The marina is the heart of the district and is backed by apartments that once housed the athletes from the games. Sleek and expensive yachts and boats of all shapes and sizes line the pontoons. The enclosed marina, and the nearby promenades, are lined with bars and restaurants of all descriptions. Inland, the tallest buildings are the Mapfre towers and the opulent Hotel Arts, part of a development that had almost as big an impact on Barcelona as the 19th-century construction of the Eixample.

Fun in the sun To either side of Port Olímpic lie clean, sandy beaches, attracting both visitors and Barcelonins. The beaches stretch north from Barceloneta to the Museu Blau (▷ 105), which was built to host a "cultural Olympics" in 2004. Spruced up in the late 1980s, the esplanade is 8km (5 miles) long, and is backed by tree-lined grassy spaces, offering cyclists, roller-bladers and strollers an escape from the city. Along with water sports and beach games, you'll find freshwater showers, sunbed rental, children's playparks and all you need for a day at the beach. When the sun sets there are the *xiringuitos* (beach bars) and restaurants in the Port Olímpic to refresh and revive.

THE BASICS

➕ K9
✉ Port Olímpic
🚇 Ciutadella–Vila Olímpica
🚌 39, 51, H14, H16

HIGHLIGHTS

● Frank Gehry's *Lobster* sculpture
● Strolling or cycling the Passeig Marítim
● El Fòrum (Forum complex)
● Sandy beaches

Port Vell

HIGHLIGHTS

● A meal or drink overlooking the marina
● Harbour trip on one of the *golondrinas* pleasure boats (lasgolondrinas.com)
● The Aquàrium

TIPS

● There's a craft market at the weekends near the Palau del Mar overlooking the Port Vell.
● Sundays are very busy, so watch your valuables.
● Shops in Maremagnum are open Sunday.

The best way to reach the lively Old Port area is by strolling along the undulating wooden Rambla de Mar boardwalk across the water to the Maremagnum leisure complex and Aquarium.

Back to the sea Barcelona has often been accused of ignoring the sea on which much of its prosperity depended. In the past, the closest most tourists came to it was an ascent of the 60m (200ft) Monument a Colom (commemorating the return of Columbus from the New World in 1493) at the seaward end of the Ramblas. Now, Port Vell is given over to pleasure and entertainment and most shipping activity takes place at the modern port installations to the west, although ferries to the Balearics still depart from here.

Clockwise from far left: the Rambla de Mar walkway; the Maremagnum complex at night and by day; the Aquàrium; one of the *golondrina pleasure boats*

Peninsula The Maremagnum, a huge covered shopping and entertainment complex at the heart of the Old Port, is connected to the main-land by the Rambla de Mar, which is usually thronged with tourists. The area is particularly appealing in summer, when you want a sea breeze, and at night, when everything is brilliantly illuminated and some of the restaurants and bars are worth checking out. The shopping mall in the Maremagnum is very good, while outside you'll find the Aquàrium, which is one of the largest in Europe (allow a couple of hours for a visit). Take a walk through the 80m long (265ft) glass tunnel to experience sharks swimming a few inches from your face. Barcelona's *golondrinas* (swallowboats) offer trips from the Port Vell quayside. Trips also tour the harbour and the coastline.

THE BASICS

Aquàrium
aquariumbcn.com

🔒 G9

✉ Moll d'Espanya

☎ 93 221 74 74

🕐 Open daily, but hours vary widely. Jun–Sep 10–10; check website for rest of year

Ⓜ Drassanes

🚌 59, 120, D20, H14, V11, V13

💰 Expensive

Monument a Colom

🔒 F/G8

✉ Plaça del Portal de la Pau

☎ 93 302 52 24

🕐 Daily 8.30–8

Ⓜ Barceloneta, Drassanes

🚌 D20, H14, V11

💰 Moderate

Santa Maria del Mar

HIGHLIGHTS

Santa Maria
● Rose window in west front
In the Ribera
● Passeig del Born with central Rambla
● 19th-century glass-and-iron Born Market building
● Fosser de les Moreres square
● Medieval houses in Carrer Montcada

TIP

● The best time to visit is during the afternoon on a weekday, when there are fewer services.

A fortress of the faith in the old waterfront area of the Ribera, the Church of Our Lady of the Sea is one of the greatest expressions of Catalan Gothic. It was built on the proceeds of Barcelona's maritime supremacy in the Middle Ages.

The Ribera Literally "the seaside" or "waterfront", the Ribera was the city's hub in the 13th century, when Catalan commerce dominated the Western Mediterranean ports. Successful merchants and entrepreneurs set themselves up in fine town houses close to the busy shore, cheek by jowl with workers, dock porters and craftspeople. The street names of the Ribera still reflect the trades once practised here: Assaonadors (tanners), Espaseria (swordmaking) and Argenteria (silversmithing).

Clockwise from far left: a statue bathed in sunlight; detail of a stained-glass window; the austere exterior of the church of Santa Maria del Mar

People's church Santa Maria was begun in 1329, the foundation stone commemorating the Catalan conquest of Sardinia. It has always been a popular church, the focus of this once busy port district; the whole population is supposed to have toiled on the church's construction for 50 years. The life of the Ribera is reflected in decorative touches such as delightful depictions of dock workers on the doors and the altar. The altar is crowned by a wooden model of a 15th-century ship. Other than that, the interior of the church is almost bare; its elaborate baroque furnishings were torched during the Civil War, though the glorious stained-glass windows survived. Now the calm and symmetry created by its high vaults and by the majestic spacing of its octagonal columns can be appreciated without distraction.

THE BASICS

➕ H8

✉ Plaça de Santa Maria

☎ 93 310 23 90

🕐 Mon–Sat 9–1.30, 4.30–8, Sun 10–1, 4.30–8; guided tours in English daily 2, 3, 5.15

🚇 Jaume 1

🚌 45, 51, 120, H14, V15, V17

♿ Good (near entrance)

💶 Free; guided tours moderate

More to See

EL BORN CENTRE DE CULTURA I MEMÒRIA

elbornculturaimemoria.barcelona.cat

While this former covered market was being converted into a cultural centre, the ruins of a swathe of the city that had been destroyed to make way for the Ciutadella fortress were discovered. These now form the centrepiece of an exhibition on the 1714 siege of Barcelona.

➕ H8 ✉ Plaça Comercial 12 ☎ 93 256 68 51 🕓 Mar–Oct daily 10–8, Nov–Feb Mon–Fri 10–7, Sat–Sun 10–8 🚇 Jaume 1 💷 Exhibition inexpensive, ruins free

MUSEU DE CULTURES DEL MÓN

museuculturesmon.bcn.cat

Set in two adjoining Gothic palaces, this atmospheric museum displays remarkable artworks from cultures across the globe, from pre-Columbian objects from the Andes to Japanese paintings.

➕ H8 ✉ Carrer Montcada 12 ☎ 93 256 23 00 🕓 Tue–Sat 10–7, Sun 10–8 💷 Inexpensive, free Sun after 3pm

MUSEU DE LA XOCOLATA

museuxocolata.cat

In this museum devoted to chocolate, you'll find an overview of the history of chocolate from its New World origins to its arrival in Europe. There are staggering chocolate creations and a tempting shop.

➕ H8 ✉ Carrer del Comerç 36 ☎ 93 268 78 78 🕓 Mon–Sat 10–7 (Jul–Aug till 8), Sun 10–3 🚇 Jaume 1 💷 Moderate

ZOO BARCELONA

zoobarcelona.cat

In the Parc de la Ciutadella (▷ 66), the zoo has more than 400 species, but its reputation lies in the primates. Many are in danger of extinction, notably the Bornean orangutan and the mangabey, the world's smallest monkeys. Other fast-disappearing animals include the Iberian wolf. There's also a children's petting zoo.

➕ J8 ☎ 902 457 545 🕓 Jun–Sep daily 10–7; mid-Mar to May, Oct daily 10–6; Jan to mid-Mar, Nov–Dec daily 10–5 🚇 Barceloneta, Arc de Triomf 💷 Expensive

Gorillas and eastern bongos are two of the species you can see at Zoo Barcelona

La Ribera

You can experience the full range of the Born's architecture and soak up the atmosphere on this walk in the Ribera.

DISTANCE: 2km (1.2 miles) **ALLOW:** 60 minutes

START

END

PLAÇA DE SANTA MARIA DEL MAR
▷ 70 ✚ H8 🚇 Jaume I

PLAÇA DE SANTA MARIA DEL MAR
🚇 Jaume I

❶ Walk to the right of the Basilica de Santa Maria del Mar and continue onto Carrer de Santa Maria. Continue to the end to the back of the church.

❽ Turn right onto Carrer dels Canvis Vells. At the end of the road is the Plaça de Santa Maria del Mar.

❷ Turn left, crossing over the Placeta de Montcada and into the Carrer de Montcada. At the end of Carrer de Montcada turn right onto Carrer de la Princesa.

❼ Take Carrer del Bonaire out of the square, which further on changes its name to Carrer del Consolat de Mar. Stop when you reach the intersection with Carrer dels Canvis Vells on your right.

❸ Continue to the end of Carrer de la Princesa to Parc de la Ciutadella and Museu de Ciències Naturals. Turn right onto Passeig de Picasso and follow the perimeter of the park for one block.

❻ Turn left onto Carrer de Palau, which brings you to the charming Plaça de les Olles, a small square with outdoor cafés and apartment blocks with pretty facades.

❹ Turn right onto Carrer de la Fusina and then left onto Carrer del Comerç. Here you walk around the facade of the former Mercat del Born, now a cultural centre (▷ 72).

❺ With your back to the market, keep left, following Carrer del Comerç to the intersection with Avinguda del Marquès de l'Argentera.

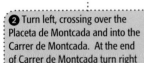

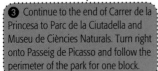

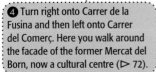

Shopping

ALAMACEN MARABI

almacenmarabi.blogspot.co.uk
These handmade felt toys aren't cheap, but their quality and sheer charm are priceless. Kids will love the large animals and teddy bears and there are smaller items, such as finger puppets, which make unique gifts.

⊞ H8 ✉ Carrer de la Cirera 6 🚇 Jaume I

BARAKA

barakaweb.com
There is plenty to tempt you from Morocco in this small shop: handcrafted silver jewellery, brass lamps, *catifes* (woven rugs) and dainty *babuchas* (leather slippers).

⊞ H8 ✉ Carrer Canvis Vells 2 ☎ 93 268 42 20 🚇 Jaume I, Barceloneta

BEATRIZ FUREST

beatrizfurest.com
Beatriz Furest's exquisitely designed bags and purses are timeless and regularly feature on the pages of fashion magazines. A small selection of shoes, scarves and belts round out the line.

⊞ H8 ✉ Carrer Esparteria 1 ☎ 93 268 37 96 🚇 Barceloneta, Jaume I

BUBÓ

bubo.es
Carles Mampel makes chocolate bonbons, cakes and other goodies, which he carefully displays in this chocolate boutique with the reverence of fine jewellery. Next door there is a café where you can taste before buying.

⊞ H8 ✉ Carrer Caputxes 10 ☎ 93 268 72 24 🚇 Jaume I

CASA GISPERT

casagispert.com
An expert roaster of nuts and coffees, this establishment sells everything from fresh-roasted hazelnuts and almonds to Iranian pistachios.

⊞ H8 ✉ Carrer de Sombrerers 23 ☎ 93 319 75 35 🚇 Jaume I

LA COMERCIAL

lacomercial.info
Born is full of little shops selling designer goods for the home, but La Comercial is perhaps the most appealing. Whether you want a Diptyque candle, a trendy cushion or a fabulous rug, you're bound to find it here. Five nearby branches sell fashion.

⊞ H8 ✉ Carrer Bonaire 4 ☎ 93 295 46 30 🚇 Barceloneta, Jaume I

COQUETTE

coquettebcn.com
This gorgeous boutique, which has a huge mother-of-pearl chandelier cascading from the ceiling, offers a chic and understated range of womenswear from labels such as Intropia and Isabel Marant Étoile. Menswear is around the corner at Carrer Bonaire 5.

⊞ H8 ✉ Carrer del Rec 65 ☎ 93 319 29 76 🚇 Barceloneta, Jaume I

DEMASIÉ

demasie.es
This artisan bakery's specializes in swirly pastries—not just their signature

---

FINE DESIGN

Barcelona's design tradition and its array of unusual and individual shops make hunting for gifts and accessories a real pleasure. Fine leather goods at reasonable prices can be found everywhere in the Eixample, and there are numerous expensive jewellery shops. In the Old Town, look for hand-painted jewellery, ceramics, textiles and crafts.

cinnamon roll, but other flavours such as blueberry, matcha tea or maple and pecan. They also offer giant cookies and cupcakes.

⊞ H8 ⊠ Carrer Princesa 28 ☎ 93 304 03 00 Ⓜ Jaume I

GIDLÖÖF

gidloof.com

This large, loft-style space contains classic Scandinavian antiques and vintage goodies, lovingly restored by the owners. Classic designs, such as Mathsson chairs and metal bookcases by String, feature, along with their own furniture and textile collections.

⊞ H8 ⊠ Passatge Mercantil 1, Born ☎ 93 368 22 25 Ⓜ Barceloneta, Jaume I

MAREMAGNUM

maremagnum.es

Best approached via the Rambla de Mar so you can appreciate the spectacular mirror canopy over the entrance, this shopping centre is open every day of the year. As well as international chains and boutiques, there are cafés, restaurants and bars.

⊞ G9 ⊠ Moll d'Espanya ☎ 93 225 81 00 Ⓜ Drassanes

MERCAT DE SANTA CATERINA

mercatsantacaterina.net

The range, variety and quality of the produce here reflects the area's wealth, with everything from meat, fish and vegetables to flowers, imported groceries and luxury chocolates on offer.

⊞ H7 ⊠ Avinguda Francesc Cambò 16 ☎ 93 319 57 40 Ⓜ Jaume I

MINU MADHU

Come here for a superb range of shawls, scarves and elegant silk jackets; scarves range from traditional fringed

silk to pashminas, woollen wraps and lace and gossamer silk for evening wear.

⊞ H8 ⊠ Carrer de Santa Maria 18 ☎ 93 310 27 85 Ⓜ Jaume I

ON LAND

on-land.com

Find urban fashion for men and women in Josep Abril's shop, which sells his own designs and labels such as Montse Ibanez and Petit Bateau; T-shirts by Divinas Palabras are a good buy.

⊞ H8 ⊠ Carrer Princesa 25 18 ☎ 93 310 02 11 Ⓜ Jaume I

LE SWING

leswingvintage.com

This charming boutique specializes in vintage clothing (including pieces from labels such as Chanel and Versace). Velvet gowns, beaded bags, and frothy frocks are elegantly displayed, alongside vintage jewellery and sunglasses.

⊞ H8 ⊠ Plaça del Rec 16 ☎ 93 310 14 49 Ⓜ Jaume I

VILA VINITECA

vilaviniteca.es

The number one shop for wine connoisseurs supplies many of the city's top restaurants. The selection is so vast it can be overwhelming, but the staff are very helpful. They sell gourmet produce in their shop next door.

⊞ H8 ⊠ Carrer Agullers 7 ☎ 90 232 77 77 Ⓜ Jaume 1

WAWAS

This has all the usual souvenirs—postcards, mugs, magnets, T-shirts—but you won't find any of the standard tourist tat. These stylish and witty designs make ideal gifts to take home.

⊞ H8 ⊠ Carrer Carders 14 ☎ 93 319 79 92 Ⓜ Jaume I

Entertainment and Nightlife

C.D.L.C.

cdlcbarcelona.com

The nightspot of the see-and-be-seen crowd has Bedouin-style "boudoirs" lining the edge of the dance floor, two bars and a restaurant, right at the water's edge.

➕ J9 ✉ Passeig Marítim 32 ☎ 93 224 04 70 🕐 Daily noon–2.30am 🚇 Ciutadella–Vila Olímpica

ECLIPSE

eclipse-barcelona.com

On the 26th floor of the W Hotel, this smooth-as-silk bar has a staggering view of the coastline. Try their signature vodka and passion fruit cocktail.

➕ Off map G8 ✉ Plaça Rosa de les Vents 1 ☎ 93 295 28 00 🕐 Sun–Thu 6pm–2am, Fri–Sat 6pm–3am 🚇 Barceloneta

MAGIC CLUB

magic-club.net

A long-running city institution, Magic remains one of the only rock-themed discos in Barcelona. There are two dance floors and it hosts live gigs as well as club nights.

➕ H8 ✉ Passeig Picasso 40 ☎ 93 310 12 67 🕐 Thu–Sat and night before public hols 11pm–6am 🚇 Jaume I

JAZZ ROOTS

Barcelona's love affair with jazz goes back to before the Civil War, when Jack Hylton's dance band played at the International Exhibition and Django Reinhardt and Stéphane Grappelli brought the music of the Hot Club de France to the Hot Club de Barcelone. The tradition has been kept alive by a continual influx of American jazz musicians, including saxophonist Bill McHenry, and by the city's annual Jazz Festival (mid-Oct to mid-Nov).

PAU CASALS

The great cellist, better known to the world as Pablo Casals (1876–1973), was a Catalan. In 1920, he helped push Barcelona onto Europe's musical map by founding his Barcelona Orchestra, which performed regularly in the Palau de la Música. In 1924–25, Igor Stravinsky directed the orchestra in concerts featuring his own works.

PALAU DE LA MÚSICA CATALANA

palaumusica.cat

Domènech i Montaner's Palace of Music has long been Barcelona's principal auditorium, a splendid setting for performances by European classical ensembles and visiting jazz artists.

➕ H7 ✉ Carrer Sant Francesc de Paula 2 ☎ 902 475 485 🚇 Urquinaona

RAZZMATAZZ

salarazzmatazz.com

Five nightclubs and top-notch live music venue (especially for indie and electronica) make this the place to party.

➕ K7 ✉ Carrer de Pamplona 88 ☎ 93 320 82 00 🕐 Fri–Sat 1am–6am 🚇 Bogatell

SHÔKO

shoko.biz

This elegant, Ibiza-style club by the sea plays 80s funk during the week and house music on the weekends.

➕ J9 ✉ Passeig Marítim 36 ☎ 93 225 92 00 🕐 Daily noon–3am 🚇 Cuitadella–Vila Olímpica

EL XAMPANYET

This traditional little bar can always be relied on for a lively crowd, good-value tapas and their specialty, a house cava. The best place to sit is at the zinc bar.

➕ H8 ✉ Carrer Montcada 22 ☎ 93 319 70 03 🕐 Tue–Sat 12–4, 7–11 🚇 Jaume I

PRICES
Prices are approximate, based on a 3-course meal for one person.
€€€ over €50
€€ €25–€50
€ under €25

AGUA (€€)

grupotragaluz.com/en/restaurant/agua/
Watch the waves while you eat at this modern, laid-back restaurant near the Port Olímpic, where dishes range from tasty seafood to traditional Catalan fare.
➕ J9 ✉ Passeig Marítim 30 ☎ 93 225 12 72 🕐 Sun–Thu noon–11.30, Fri–Sat noon–12.30am 🚇 Ciutadella Vila–Olímpica

EL ATRIL (€)

atrilbarcelona.com
For bistro-style food at fair prices, this cosy eatery with outdoor terrace in the Sant Pere district is a good choice. The mussels and *pommes frites* are particularly good, and there's an international menu. It does a great Sunday brunch.
➕ H7 ✉ Carrer Carders 23 ☎ 93 310 12 20 🕐 Daily noon–midnight 🚇 Jaume I

BESTIAL (€€)

grupotragaluz.com/restaurante/bestial/
Arguably the best seaside terrace in Barcelona, with wood decking on several levels and parasols, Bestial offers Italian fare at reasonable prices.
➕ J9 ✉ Carrer de Ramon Trias Fargas 2–4 ☎ 93 224 04 07 🕐 Daily 1–4, 8–midnight 🚇 Ciutadella–Vila Olímpica

LA BOMBETA (€)

Escape the tourist crowd at this old-fashioned tapas bar tucked away down a side street. The house specialty is *bombas*: giant, fluffy croquettes topped with a spicy *brava* sauce. It's usually packed and noisy but great fun.
➕ H9 ✉ Carrer Maquinista 3 ☎ 93 319 94 45 🕐 Mon–Sat 12.30–4, 8–1, Sun 12.30–4 🚇 Barceloneta

EL CANGREJO LOCO (€€)

elcangrejoloco.com/inicio.php
The crowds testify to the appeal of the Crazy Crab, a large Port Olímpic seafood establishment. Dining is on three levels, and the top floor has a sea view.
➕ K9 ✉ Moll de Gregal, Port Olímpic ☎ 93 221 17 48 🕐 Daily 1pm–1am 🚇 Ciutadella–Vila Olímpica

CAN SOLÉ (€€)

restaurantcansole.com
This elegant old eating house is tiled and decorated with photos of former famous patrons. Join the regulars to enjoy superb paellas, sticky-fresh fish, lobsters and plates of sweet shrimp and prawns while watching the action in the frenetic open kitchen.
➕ H9 ✉ Carrer des Sant Carles 4 ☎ 93 221 50 12 🕐 Tue–Sat 1.30–4, 8.30–11, Sun 1.30–4 🚇 Barceloneta

CASA DELFÍN (€)

tallerdetapas.com/esp/casa-delfin/
In the heart of El Born, pretty Casa Delfín has a mezzanine floor, wooden furniture and quirky wall art. Catalan classics are served, but Britannia rules in

FISH FOR ALL
The seafood restaurants of Barcelona, concentrated in bayside Barceloneta, are famous. They serve *zarsuela* (a seafood stew) and *suquet de peix* (fish-and-potato soup), as well as *fideuà* (a paella-style dish with noodles instead of rice). *Arròs negre* is rice cooked in the black ink of a squid.

the dessert menu. If you are craving an Eton Mess or toffee pudding, here's your chance.

H8 ✉ Passeig del Born 36 ☎ 93 319 50 88 🕐 Mon–Thu 8am–midnight, Fri–Sat 8am–1am 🚇 Barceloneta, Jaume I

EUSKAL ETXEA (€)

gruposagardi.com/restaurante/euskal-etxea-taberna

For authentic regional cooking, come and join the exiles from the Basque country at their cultural centre, which serves an outstanding selection of *pintxos* (tapas) from this northern region. Expect superb seafood, tender octopus, Basque cheeses and smoked meats in a cosy, dark little bar.

H8 ✉ Plaçeta de Montcada 1–3 ☎ 93 310 21 85 🕐 Daily 1–4, 7–midnight 🚇 Jaume I

GREEN SPOT (€€)

encompaniadelobos.com/the-green-spot

A chic, spacious restaurant, this serves an excellent menu of creative vegetarian and vegan dishes, from Mediterranean classics to stir-fries and curries. There's live music on Thursday evenings.

H8 ✉ Carrer de la Reina Cristina 2 ☎ 93 802 55 65 🕐 Daily 12.30–midnight 🚇 Barceloneta

KAIKU (€€)

restaurantkaiku.cat

Kaiku has a maritime-themed interior and serves a surprisingly creative menu focusing on seafood. Come early to get a spot on the terrace by the beach. The signature dish is a fabulous paella made with smoked rice (*arròs a la xef*), and they also do delicious desserts.

Off map at H9 ✉ Plaça del Mar 1 ☎ 93 221 90 82 🕐 Tue–Sun 1–3.30, 7–10.30 🚇 Barceloneta

LA PARADETA (€€)

laparadeta.com/en/

The form here is to buy a drink, inspect the mounds of mussels, clams, squid and crab and specify what you want, how you'd like it cooked and your choice of sauce. Then sit at one of the refectory tables and wait till your number's called to collect your plate.

H8 ✉ Carrer Comercial 7 ☎ 93 268 19 39 🕐 Tue–Sun 1–4, 8–11.30 🚇 Arc de Triomf, Barceloneta

SENYOR PARELLADA (€€)

senyorparellada.com

An elegant and inviting restaurant with low lighting and chandeliers, this offers refined Catalan cuisine, with dishes such as truffle-stuffed *canelones* and seafood stew. There are good set menus available, unusually for both lunch and dinner.

H8 ✉ Carrer de l'Argenteria 37 ☎ 93 310 50 94 🕐 Daily 1–4, 8–11.30 🚇 Jaume 1

SET PORTES (€€€)

7portes.com/en/

Founded in 1836 in Port Vell, the Seven Doors is one of Barcelona's most famous and reliable restaurants, serving up superb paella, fish and seafood, often made to historic recipes.

H8 ✉ Passeig d'Isabel II 14 ☎ 93 319 30 33 🕐 Daily 1–1 🚇 Barceloneta

TIPS AND TAXES

There is no fixed rule for tipping in restaurants and bars. If you have a coffee and snack, leave change rounded up to the nearest euro. In all restaurants a 7 per cent VAT tax (called IVA) is added to bills, but this should not be confused with a service charge. If a full meal is served, leave 5–10 per cent, though in cheaper tapas bars a euro or two should suffice.

L'Eixample

Largely built as the city expanded in the 19th century, L'Eixample (the Extension) is a grid-patterned urban area, bisected by the arrow-straight Diagonal. It's home to the city's finest *modernista* buildings.

Sights	**82–92**
Walk	**93**
Shopping	**94–95**
Entertainment and Nightlife	**96**
Where to Eat	**97–98**

2

Park Güell

LA SALUT

Baixada Repartidor
Casa-Museu
Gaudí
C de la Gloria
Verdi
C de Sostres
Carrer d'Olot

C Albigesos
C Valldoreix
Carrer St
Larrard
Rbla Mercedes
Molist
C Maignon
Sant Josep
de la Muntanya
Cugat del Vallès

**PLAÇA
DE LESSEPS**
● Lesseps

3

TRAVESSERA

GRÀCIA

C Nil Fabra
C M Serrahima
C Galdós
IOLLA
C la Granja
Carrer
del
Cardener
C Flors
C Salvador
L'ESCORIAL

Casa
Vicens
C Carolines
Betlem
Museu
S Grácia
Topazi
C Santa Agata
C Sta Rosa
C Blada
C Tília
C Mateu
C del Carrer
Rob
d'Asturies
Viada
Plaça del
Nord
Alzina
C Villafranca
Massens
Rabassa
Martí
C de la Legalitat

Fontana ●
Carrer
Plaça del
Diamant
Tres C Senyores
Congost
C de la Legalitat
C de l'Alegre

C Berga
C del
C de l'Or
C la
Plaça de la
Virreina
Blanques
Torrent
Carrer
C de St Lluis

C del Cigne
Montseny
C la
Perla
Torlfos
Vallfogona
Plaça
d'En Joanic
C H Lázaro

Plaça
Llibertat
C Ros
C de Olano
C Planeta
C Maspons
Teroi
C del Montmany
C Bruniquer
Joanic ●
CARRER
de St

GRAN
C Pere
C Ramón
C y
Cajal

TRAVESSERA DE GRÀCIA
TRAVESSERA

L Antúnez
C Goya
C Diluvi
Puigmartí
Plaça
N Oller
C Riera de
C Mozart
C M de la Rosa
Siracusa
de
Tordera
C Quevedo
JOAN
C Flor
C Grassot
DE

4

5

C Neptú
C Mineva
C Seneca
C Fco Giner
C Progrés
C Fraternitat
C de la Llibertat
C Igualada
BAILEN
CARRER
C d'En
CARRER
DE
C Nápols

C Torres
C Monistrol
C Roger

C Bonavista
C del
Perill
Casa
Comalat
CÒRSEGA
C Girona
de

P Carrer de
Còrsega
CARRER
Casa de
les Punxes
CARRER
PLAÇA
MOSSÈN JACINT
VERDAGUER
Palau
Robert
AVINGUDA
Verdaguer ●

Carrer del
Rosselló
Diagonal
CATALUNYA
PLAÇA JOAN
CARLES
DIAGONAL

La Pedrera ●
Provença

Provença ●
Carrer
de
GRÀCIA
Casa
Thomas
MALLORCA

P Centre
Català d'Art
BALMES
DE
Museu
Egipci
CLARIS
LLÚRIA
PAU
VALÈNCIA
ROGER
FLOR

CARRER
Fundació
Antoni Tàpies
DE
D'ARAGÓ

6

Museu del
Perfum
CARRER
Passeig
de Gràcia
Museu del
Modernisme
RAMBLA
Mansana de
la Discòrdia
PASSEIG
Carrer
del
Consell
de Cent
BRUC
DEL
Girona
Carrer
BAILEN
PASSEIG
ROGER
DE
**Universitat
de Barcelona**
Carrer
de
la
Diputació

Passeig
de Gràcia ●
GRAN
VIA
DE
**PLAÇA DE
TETUAN**
Tetuan
LES

0 ————— 250 m
0 ————— 250 yds

G   **H**

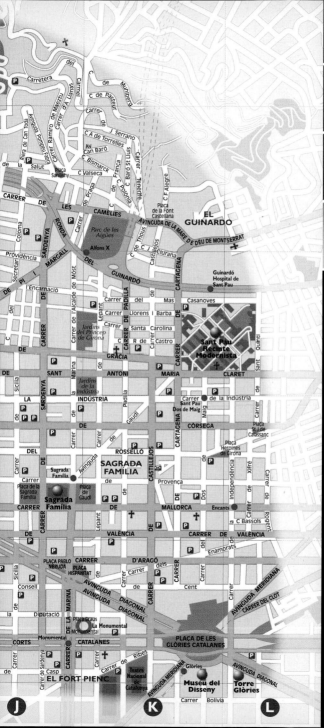

J K L

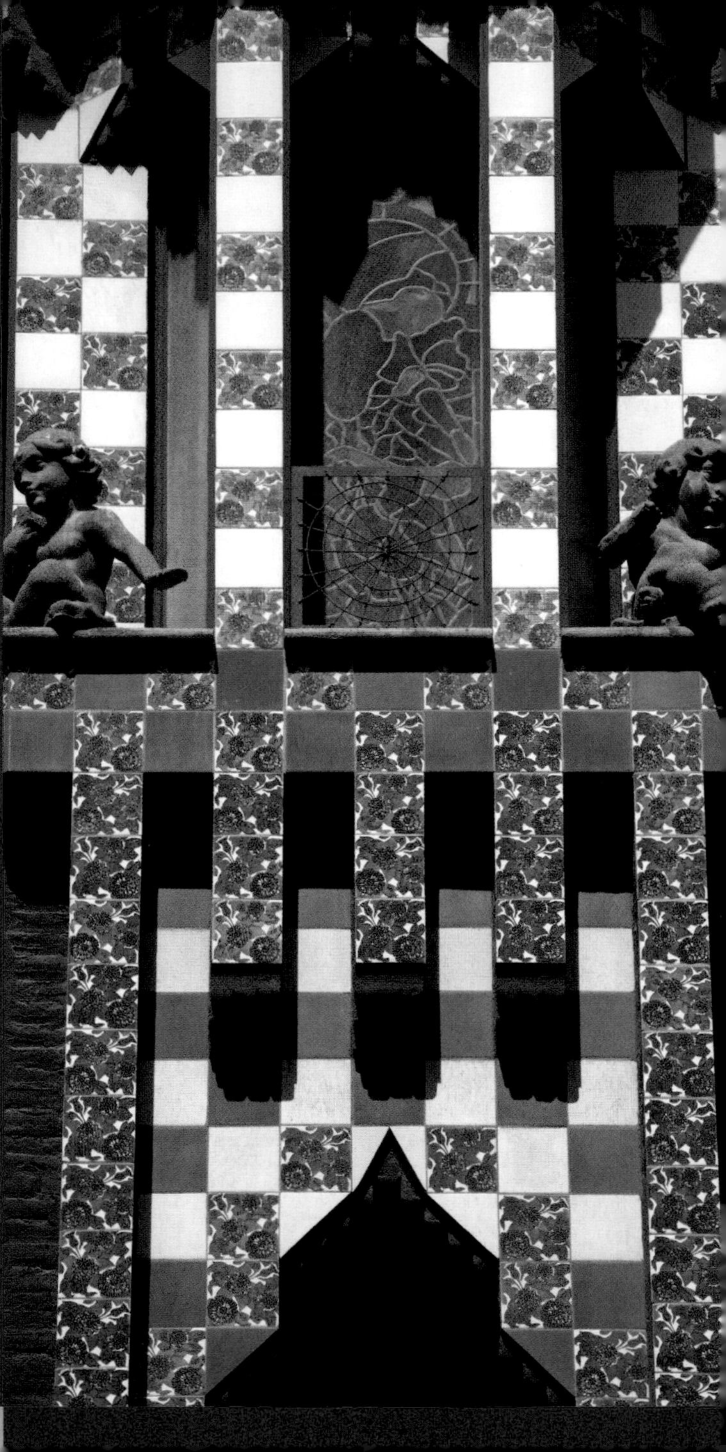

You'll find peaceful squares, lively bars and a seven-day street party in this distinctive neighbourhood. It's home to the Park Güell and Casa Vicens.

Cultural village Originally a collection of tiny farms, Gràcia grew rapidly in the 19th century, becoming part of Barcelona itself in 1897. Gràcia was renowned then as a cultural and political hub, and this is reflected in some street names—Mercat de la Libertat and Plaça de la Revolució. It was also a place where music and theatre thrived and today there are cultural spaces of all kinds.

Graceful Gràcia Apart from the Park Güell (▷ 86–87), the pick of Gràcia attractions are Gaudí's first house, the exquisite Casa Vicens (opened to the public in 2017), and Lluís Domènech i Montaner's Casa Fuster, now a hotel. *Plaças* such as Virreina, Sol and Vila de Gràcia are attractive places to pause or stop for a coffee during the day. Boasting some of the best bars and restaurants in the city, Gràcia comes into its own at night.

Summer festival The *Festa Major* has taken place annually for more than 150 years. For seven days during the second half of August, it takes over Gràcia. Each street puts up a display, with themes ranging from the Wild West to the Civil War, and the suburb is a riot of colour. You'll also find music and plays peformed outdoors on the various *plaças*.

THE BASICS

✚ G/H4

🍴 Many restaurants and bars

🚇 Fontana, Gràcia, Joanic

🚌 22, 24, 28, 39, 55

Casa Vicens

⬆ G3

✉ Carrer de les Carolines 20–26

☎ 93 547 59 80

🕐 Daily 10–8

🚻 Good

✋ Expensive

HIGHLIGHTS

Casa Vicens
● Elaborate exterior decoration
● Decorative wrought-iron gates

Casa Fuster
● Mix of neo-Gothic and classical styles
● Viennese-style ground floor café

Plaça de la Vila de Gràcia
● Bell tower, designed by Antoni Rovira i Trias

Park Güell
● Incredible tilework
● Amazing city views

Mansana de la Discòrdia

HIGHLIGHTS

No. 35
● Exterior sculptures
● Dome perched on columns

No. 41
● Sculpture of St. George and dragon by entrance
● Grotesque sculptures in third-floor windows
● Lamps and stained-glass panels in entrance

No. 43
● Chromatic designs on façade by Gaudí's collaborator, the artist Josep Maria Jujol

TIP

● The Casa Batlló is hugely popular in the mornings. Go late afternoon for a less-crowded visit.

A century ago, the bourgeoisie of Barcelona vied with each other in commissioning ever more extravagant homes. The most extraordinary of these ornament the Block of Discord on Passeig de Gràcia.

Enlivening the Eixample In an attempt to relieve the rigidity of Cerdà's grid of streets, *modernista* architects studded the Eixample with some of the most exciting urban buildings ever seen. *Modernisme*, the uniquely Catalan contribution to late 19th-century architecture, has obvious links with art nouveau, but here it also breathes the spirit of nationalism and civic pride because Barcelona was the richest city in Spain. The Mansana de la Discòrdia juxtaposes the work of three great architects of the age.

No. 35 Domènech i Montaner completed the six-floor Casa Lleó-Morera in 1905. Much of this corner building was destroyed during improvements in the 1940s, but its striking *modernista* style and curved balconies have survived.

No. 41 Built in 1898 by Puig i Cadafalch, the Casa Amatller has an internal courtyard and staircase like the medieval palaces along Carrer Montcada. Outside, it is a wonderful mixture of Catalan Gothic and Flemish Renaissance, faced with bright tiles and topped by a big gable.

No. 43 The Casa Batlló reflects the hand of Antoni Gaudí, who restyled the house in 1906. It is said to represent the triumph of St. George over the dragon with its heaving roof, scaly skin of mosaic tiles, windows and tower.

THE BASICS

casabatllo.es
amatller.org

✚ G6

✉ Passeig de Gràcia 35, 41, 43

☎ Casa Batlló: 93 216 03 06; Casa Amatller: 93 461 74 60

🕐 Casa Batlló: daily 9–9, last admission 8pm; Casa Amatller: daily 10–6, visit by guided tour only— in English daily at 11

🚇 Passeig de Gràcia

🚌 7, 16, 17, 22, 24, 28

♿ Fair

✋ Expensive

Park Güell

HIGHLIGHTS

● Dragon at entrance
to park
● Curved and tiled benches
on main square
● Entrance pavilions
● Ironwork of entrance
gates
● Palm-like stonework of
buttresses
● Leaning pillars of arcade
● *Modernista* furnishings
in Casa Museu Gaudí

TIP

● The park is a 15-minute
uphill walk from the metro
(assisted by escalators)
and the only bus that stops
outside is the No. 24; use
the Bus Turístic if you have
a ticket.

**Antoni Gaudí's passion for natural forms
was given full rein when he turned his
hand to landscape design, creating this
extraordinary hilltop park with its brightly
coloured, flowing architectural shapes.**

Unfulfilled intentions The rocky ridge, which
has a magnificent view of Barcelona and the
Mediterranean, was bought in 1895 by Gaudí's
rich patron, Eusebi Güell, with the idea of devel-
oping an English-style garden city (hence the
British spelling of "park". The project flopped;
only three houses were built, and the area was
taken over by the city council as a park in 1923.

Monumental Zone The central part of the park
that contains all the Gaudí sculptures (officially
known as the Monumental Zone) is dominated

Clockwise from far left: animal mosaic; the main staircase; the Sala Hipóstila; the swirls of benches in the Gran Plaça

by a great terrace, supported on a forest of neo-Grecian columns and bounded by a sinuous balustrade-cum-bench whose form was allegedly copied from the imprint left by a human body in a bed of plaster; the surface is covered by fragments of bright ceramic tiles. The strange space beneath the terrace was intended to be a market; it gapes cavernlike at the top of the steps leading from the park's main entrance.

Surreal landscape A ceramic serpent slithers down the stairway toward the main entrance, which is guarded by two peculiar gingerbread-style buildings with bulbous roofs. Gaudí scattered other idiosyncratic details through the park, sucha as steps and serpentine paths. In his later years, he lived in the house built by his pupil Francesc Berenguer, now the Casa Museu Gaudí.

THE BASICS

parkguell.cat
⊞ H/J2
✉ Carrer d'Olot
☎ 93 213 04 88
⏱ Monumental Zone: Apr–Oct daily 8.30–8.30; Nov–Mar daily 8.30–6.30. Casa Museu Gaudí: Apr–Sep daily 9–8; Oct–Mar daily 10–6
🍴 Café
Ⓜ Vallcarca, Lesseps
🚌 24, 87 ♿ Few
♿ Monumental Zone and Casa Museu Gaudí moderate; rest of park free

HIGHLIGHTS

● Ground-floor entrance's wall and ceiling paintings
● Rooftop
● El Pis de Pedrera: an apartment decorated with *modernista* furniture in situ
Espai Gaudí
● Audiovisual show
● Plans and models of major buildings
● Stereofunicular model of building structure
● Gaudí souvenir shop (separate entrance)

TIP

● During July and August jazz concerts are held on the roof. Enquire about dates and times at the ticket office.

"Get a violin" was architect Gaudí's response to a resident who wondered where to install a grand piano in this coral reef of an apartment block, which is very short on conventional straight lines.

Casa Mila Anecdotes about the building abound: the artist Santiago Rusinyol is supposed to have said that a snake would be a more suitable pet here than a dog. Lampooned for decades after its completion in 1912, this extraordinary building was restored and opened to visitors in 1990. Nicknamed La Pedrera (stone quarry), it was built for Pere Milà Camps, a rich industrialist who afterward complained that Gaudí's extravagance had reduced him to penury. The steel frame that supports the seven-floor structure is completely concealed

Clockwise from far left: the dramatic staircase in La Pedrera; close-up detail of an elaborate chimney; the facade; overview of the chimneys; the "centurions"

behind an undulating outer skin of stone bedecked with balconies whose encrustations of ironwork resemble floating fronds of seaweed. Obscured from the street, the rooftop undulates too, and is scattered with clusters of chimneys that resemble Roman centurions.

Gaudí the innovator Gaudí originally proposed a spiral ramp that would bring automobiles to the apartment doors—an impractical idea as it turned out—but La Pedrera nevertheless had one of the world's first underground garages. The building's beautifully brick-vaulted attics have become the Espai Gaudí, the best place to learn about Gaudí's life and work. Of particular interest are the interior photographs of some of the Gaudí buildings that are not normally open to the public.

THE BASICS

lapedrera.com

✚ G5

✉ Provença 261–265

☎ 90 290 21 38

🕓 Mar–Oct 9–8; Nov–Feb 9–6.30

🚇 Diagonal

🚌 7, 16, 17, 22, 24, V17

♿ Good (but not on roof)

✋ Expensive

Sagrada Família

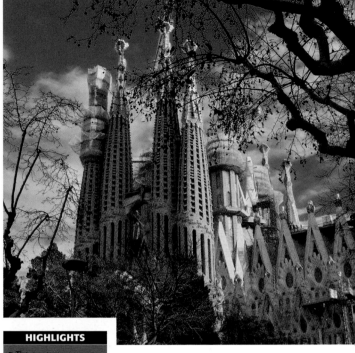

EIXAMPLE TOP 25

HIGHLIGHTS

● The museum
● Seeing artisans working in situ on the new sculptures
● Elevator or stairway into tower (not for the fearful)
● Symbolic sculptures of Nativity facade

TIPS

● Buy your tickets online in advance to avoid the massive queues.
● Cafés around the Sagrada Família are overpriced. Walk north to Avinguda Gaudí.

George Orwell thought Gaudí's great Temple of the Holy Family one of the ugliest buildings he ever saw and wondered why the Anarchists hadn't wrecked it in the Civil War. Today, it is an emblem of the city.

Devoted designer A must on every visitor's itinerary, Barcelona's most famous building is a mere fragment of what its architect intended. The ultra-pious Gaudí began work in 1883, and from 1915 dedicated himself utterly to building a temple that would do penance for the materialism of the modern world. There was never any expectation that the great structure would be completed in his lifetime; his plan called for 18 high towers dominated by an even taller one, an amazing 170m (560ft) high, dedicated to Jesus Christ.

The Nativity facade (left) was the first to be completed and was intended by Gaudí to set the tone for the rest of the building; the myriad of tall, branching columns inside the church (right) create an impression of a stone forest

Gaudí did succeed in completing one of the towers, the major part of the east (Nativity) front, the pinnacled apse and the crypt, where he camped out during the last months of his life, before he was run down and killed by a tram. Ever since, the fate of the building has been the subject of sometimes bitter controversy.

Work in progress Many Barcelonins would have preferred the church to be left as it was at Gaudí's death, a monument to its creator. During the Civil War the Anarchists destroyed Gaudí's models and drawings but spared the building. Enthusiasm for completion of the project revived in the 1950s. Work has continued, and the church was finally consecrated by Pope Benedict XVI in 2010, but with 10 towers left to go, completion is likely to take another 10 years.

THE BASICS

sagradafamilia.org

✚ J5

✉ Mallorca 401 (entrance on Carrer Sardenya)

☎ 93 208 04 14

🕐 Apr–Sep daily 9–8; Oct–Feb 9–6, Mar 9–7. Open 9–2 on 25–26 Dec, 1 and 6 Jan

🚇 Sagrada Família

🚌 19, 33, 34, 50, H10

✋ Expensive

More to See

MUSEU DEL DISSENY

ajuntament.barcelona.cat

The Design Museum occupies a bold new building in Barcelona's emerging technology district and brings together collections of textiles, ceramics and decorative arts.
✚ K6 ✉ Plaça de les Glòries 37 🕐 Tue–Sun 10–8.30 🚇 Glòries 👣 Moderate

FUNDACIÓ ANTONI TÀPIES

Antoni Tàpies is best known for his abstract art, and his earthy creations can be seen in this magnificently restored *modernista* building by Domènech i Montaner. It is topped with Tàpies' rooftop sculpture *Cloud and Chair*, an extraordinary extrusion of wire and tubing.
✚ G6 ✉ Carrer d'Aragó 255 ☎ 93 487 03 15 🕐 Tue–Sun 10–7 🚇 Passeig de Gràcia ♿ Good 👣 Moderate; Articket valid

SANT PAU RECINTE MODERNISTA

santpaubarcelona.org

Disliking the monotony of the Eixample, Domènech i Montaner defied it by aligning the buildings of Barcelona's first modern hospital at 45 degrees to its grid of streets. He designed 48 richly decorated pavilions, set in gardens and linked by underground corridors. Now beautifully renovated as the Sant Paul Modernisme Site, it can be explored it on a self-guided tour.
✚ K4 ✉ Carrer de Sant Antoni Maria Claret 167 ☎ 699 403 729 🕐 Apr–Oct Mon–Sat 9.30–6.30, Sun 9.30–2.30; Nov–Mar Mon–Sat 9.30–4.30, Sun 9.30–2.30 🚇 Sant Pau Dos de Maig 👣 Expensive

TORRE GLÒRIES

Designed by French architect Jean Nouvel for the local water company, Aigües de Barcelona (hence its original name, Torre Agbar), this bullet-shaped, glass-clad skyscraper was completed in 2005. At night, it is skilfully lit with blue, green and red lights that shine through a series of slats, creating a water-like, rippling effect visible all over the Eixample area.
✚ L6 ✉ Plaça de les Glòries s/n 🚇 Glòries

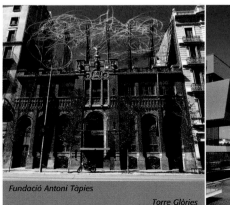

Fundació Antoni Tàpies

Torre Glòries

L'Eixample

This walk combines some fine *modernista* architecture with a stroll down one of the Eixample's major shopping thoroughfares.

DISTANCE: 2km (1.2 miles) **ALLOW:** 50 minutes

START

PLAÇA JOAN CARLES I
✚ G5 🚇 Diagonal

END

PLAÇA DE CATALUNYA
▷ 50 ✚ G7 🚇 Catalunya

❶ The first part of this walk assumes you have already seen La Pedrera (▷ 88–89) and the Mansana de la Discòrdia (▷ 84–85) and leads you past some of the lesser-known *modernista* buildings of the Eixample. Walk eastward along the Diagonal, which cuts through the area.

❻ Turn left to follow the central pedestrian promenade of Rambla de Catalunya to Plaça de Catalunya, the city's central square (▷ 50).

❷ Turn right onto Carrer de Roger de Llúria, then turn left onto Carrer de València to the medieval church and the market of La Concepció. The church was brought here piece by piece from its original site in the old town in the 19th century.

❺ Stay on the south side of Aragó to see the rooftop sculpture, *Cloud and Chair*, of the Fundació Antoni Tàpies.

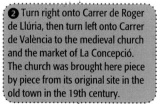

❸ Retrace your steps to Carrer de Roger de Llúria and turn left. Continue ahead and turn right onto Carrer d'Aragó.

❹ The crossing with Passeig de Gràcia gives you another chance to admire the incredible extravagances of the Mansana de la Discòrdia and to take in anything you missed first time round.

Shopping

ADOLFO DOMÍNGUEZ

adolfodominguez.com

One of Spain's brightest fashion stars, Domínguez makes clothes for men and women that manage to be mature yet achingly stylish. His "U" range caters to a more urban look.

➕ G6 ✉ Passeig de Gràcia 32 (and at other locations in the city hub) ☎ 93 487 41 70 🚇 Passeig de Gràcia

ALTAÏR

altair.es

This travel bookshop has a great range of books and maps on destinations worldwide, as well as a great café.

➕ G6 ✉ Gran Vía de les Corts Catalans 616 ☎ 93 342 71 71 🚇 Passeig de Gràcia

ANTONIO MIRO

antoniomiro.es

Miro was the first Catalan to make a name for himself in the world of fashion. His mens- and womenswear is timelessly stylish and beautifully tailored.

➕ G6 ✉ Carrer Granados 46 ☎ 93 113 26 97 🚇 Passeig de Gràcia

BAGUÉS

bagues-masriera.com/bagues

Located on the ground floor of the Casa Amatller (▷ 85), this sumptuous jewellery shop has been serving the Eixample for over 250 years. Its constantly changing collections, in which many pieces are inspired by art nouveau motifs, don't come cheap but are exquisite.

➕ G6 ✉ Passeig de Gràcia 41 ☎ 93 216 01 74 🚇 Passeig de Gràcia

BULEVARD DELS ANTIQUARIS

bulevarddelsantiquaris.com/en/

Every kind of antiques dealer can be found in this complex of more than 70 shops next to the Bulevard Rosa mall.

➕ G6 ✉ Passeig de Gràcia 55 ☎ 93 215 44 99 🚇 Passeig de Gràcia

CAMPER

camper.com

This Mallorca-based shoe brand, famous for mixing quirky style with comfort, has shops and outlets all over the city. This branch, in the Triangle shopping centre, has one of the largest ranges.

➕ G7 ✉ Carrer Pelai 13–37 ☎ 93 302 41 24 🚇 Catalunya

COLMADO QUILEZ

lafuente.es

One of Barcelona's great food stores, this continues to thrive in its new location. The shelves are stacked with a superb variety of groceries, cheeses, hams and alcohol of every description. Saffron, anchovies and coffee are sold in beautiful packaging under Quilez' own label—as is caviar, if you really want to push the boat out.

➕ G6 ✉ Rambla de Catalunya 63 ☎ 93 215 23 56 🚇 Passeig de Gràcia

DOLORES PROMESAS

dolorespromesas.com

Dolores Promesas specializes in gorgeous womenswear with a playful twist, and their flagship store here boasts a wonderful range of flirty dresses and

L'EIXAMPLE SHOPPING

playsuits with a vintage feel, as well as fun T-shirts and leisure wear.

🏠 G5 ✉ Rambla Catalunya 110 ☎ 93 496 04 61 🚇 Diagonal

ELS ENCANTS FLEA MARKET

encantsbcn.com/es

The Els Encants flea market has been running for centuries, but now occupies a striking contemporary building with mirrors and ramps. There are all kinds of stalls, from antiques to fabrics as well as mountains of junk that you can rummage through for treasures.

🏠 K6 ✉ Plaça de les Glòries ☎ 93 246 30 30 🕐 Mon, Wed, Fri, Sat 7am–9pm 🚇 Glòries

L'ILLA

lilla.com/en/

This is one of the city's larger and better *centro comerciales,* with loads of fashion, electronic and homeware shops, a supermarket and an extensive food court.

🏠 Off map ✉ Diagonal 555 🚌 6, 7, 30, 33, 34, 66, 67, 68

JAIME BERIESTAIN

beriestain.com

Jaime Beriestain, a celebrated interior designer, has a large boutique full of beautiful things for the home, from tableware to furnishings, plus a gorgeous selection of fresh flowers. Take a break from your shopping in the stylish café.

🏠 G5 ✉ Carrer Pau Claris ☎ 93 515 07 82 🚇 Diagonal

MASSIMO DUTTI

massimodutti.com

Despite the Italian-sounding name, this is a wholly Spanish fashion retailer with outlets nationwide, offering natty

designs at more than reasonable prices. Shirts are a speciality.

🏠 G4 ✉ Via Augusta 33 ☎ 93 217 73 06 🚇 Gràcia (FGC)

SANTA EULÀLIA

santaeulalia.com/es/

This prestigious emporium sells a selection of international luxury labels, such as Dior, Prada and Marc Jacobs. They also have a bespoke tailoring service and an elegant café.

🏠 G5 ✉ Passeig de Gràcia 91 ☎ 93 215 42 24 🚇 Diagonal

SEPHORA

sephora.es

This French company came up with the brilliant idea of selling top-of-the-range cosmetics and scents on supermarket merchandising principles and have never looked back.

🏠 G7 ✉ El Triangle, Carrer Pelai 13–39 ☎ 93 306 39 00 🚇 Catalunya

TOUS

tous.com

This costume jewellery and leatherwear company is known the world over. They made their mark with their iconic range of accessories featuring a teddy bear motif, but have expanded to more sophisticated pieces.

🏠 G5 ✉ Passeig de Gràcia 99 ☎ 93 488 15 58 🚇 Diagonal, Passeig de Gràcia

OUTLET FEVER

You'll find plenty of shops claiming to be "outlet" in Barcelona, but very few are actually the real thing. Exceptions are the clutch of shops along the Carrer Girona between the Gran Via and Carrer Casp. Here are fashion labels such as Mango, Nice Day and Etxart & Panno at greatly reduced prices.

Entertainment and Nightlife

ANTILLA BARCELONA

antillasalsa.com

The best of salsa and merengue guarantee good times, and free dance lessons will get you going.

➕ F6 ✉ Carrer d'Aragó 141–143 ☎ 93 451 21 51 🕐 Wed–Sat 11pm–5am, Sun 7pm–2am 🚇 Hospital Clínic

CITY HALL

cityhallbarcelona.com

Three different levels blast out a range of music from techno to house, while lounging night owls chill out on the terrace. One of downtown Barca's best places for dancing the night away.

➕ G6 ✉ Rambla de Catalunya 2–4 ☎ 93 238 07 22 🕐 Daily midnight–5am 🚇 Catalunya

DRY MARTINI

drymartiniorg.com

This elegant, ocean liner-style cocktail bar serves the best martinis in town.

➕ F5 ✉ Carrer d'Aribau 162–166 ☎ 93 217 50 72 🕐 Daily until 2.30am 🚇 Provença, Hospital Clínic, Diagonal

LES GENS QUE J'AIME

lesgensquejaime.com

This basement bar has authentic Parisian *fin de siècle* touches, and is the perfect spot for an intimate cocktail on one of the velvet settees.

➕ H5 ✉ Carrer Valencia 286 ☎ 93 215 68 79 🕐 Daily until 2.30am 🚇 Diagonal

HOTEL OMM

hotelomm.com/en/

Naturally, the city's most design-conscious hotel has its trendiest club and bar. Omm Sessions club whooshes into action in the hotel's basement, while live music can be enjoyed in the chic lobby bar.

➕ G5 ✉ Carrer Roselló 265 ☎ 93 445 40 00 🕐 Wed–Sat 11.30pm–3.30am 🚇 Diagonal

LUZ DE GAS

luzdegas.com/index.php/cat/

It's worth the journey to listen to good music in this splendidly restored old music hall. The live acts vary: jazz and blues bands grace the stage early in the week, giving way to rock, funk and Latin music on the weekends.

➕ F3 ✉ Carrer de Muntaner 246 ☎ 93 209 77 11 🚇 Muntaner (FGC)

OTTO ZUTZ

ottozutz.com/en/

This club is still the place to see and be seen for Barcelona's glitterati and those aspiring to join them. Clever lighting and metal staircases and galleries set the scene.

➕ G4 ✉ Carrer de Lincoln 15 ☎ 93 238 07 22 🕐 Wed–Sat 🚇 Gràcia

TEATRE NACIONAL DE CATALUNYA

tnc.cat

Catalonia's official public playhouse has its own resident company. Famous Spanish and international productions are staged.

➕ Off map ✉ Plaça de les Arts 1 ☎ 93 306 57 00 🚇 Glòries

XIX

xixbar.com

This unassuming bar has a USP: the best gin and tonics in town expertly mixed by Scottish barman Mike Cruikshank. You'll be lucky to get one of the small tables, though a terrace provides extra seating.

➕ E8 ✉ Carrer Rocafort 19 ☎ 93 423 43 14 🕐 Daily 6.30pm–2.30am 🚇 Rocafort

PRICES

Prices are approximate, based on a
3-course meal for one person.

€€€	over €50
€€	€25–€50
€	under €25

EL ASADOR DE BURGOS (€€€)

asadordeburgos.es

For a taste of the meat-heavy northern
Spanish diet, head for this traditional
Castilian grill house, where whole suck-
ling pigs, tender within and crackling
without, and racks of lamb are roasted
in the wood-fired oven. Superb ham
and sausages are also on the menu.
➕ H5 ✉ Carrer del Bruc 120 ☎ 93 207
31 60 🕐 Wed–Sat 12.30–midnight, Sun–Tue
12.30–5 🚇 Verdaguer

BOTAFUMEIRO (€€€)

botafumeiro.es/en/home

This spacious Galician restaurant on
Gràcia's main street serves delicious
shellfish and a selection of seafood
from the Atlantic coast.
➕ G4 ✉ Gran de Gràcia 81 ☎ 93 218 42
30 🕐 Daily noon–2am 🚇 Fontana

CACAO SAMPAKA (€)

cacaosampaka.com

This small chain specializes in quality
chocolate sold in stylish packaging and
unusual tastes. There is a rear café,
where hot chocolate is on tap and the
sandwiches and cakes are delicious.
➕ G6 ✉ Carrer Consell de Cent 292 ☎ 93
272 08 33 🕐 Mon–Sat 9–8.30 🚇 Passeig
de Gràcia

CASA CALVET (€€€)

casacalvet.es

This beautiful, modern restaurant is
housed in a Gaudí building and
specializes in cutting-edge Catalan cuisine. The service and ambience are all
you would expect in a top-class
establishment.
➕ H6 ✉ Carrer de Casp 48 ☎ 93
412 40 12 🕐 Mon–Sat 1–3.30, 8–10.30
🚇 Urquinaona

CERVECERÍA CATALANA (€)

It's generally agreed that the Cervecería
Catalana serves the widest range of
tapas in town, so getting a table here
can often require patience (they don't
take bookings). Instead grab a seat at
the bar and peruse their mouthwatering
array of morsels.
➕ G5 ✉ Carrer Mallorca 236 ☎ 93 216 03
68 🕐 Mon–Fri 8am–1.30am, Sat–Sun 9am–
1.30am 🚇 Passeig de Gracia

CHIDO ONE (€)

Crammed full of Mexican kitsch and
tequila bottles, Chido One serves
authentic dishes including mouthwatering *ceviches*, huge *burritos*, gusty *mole*
sauces and vats of fiery *salsa*.
➕ H4 ✉ Carrer de Torrijos 30 ☎ 93 285 03
35 🕐 Daily 1–10.30 🚇 Fontana

CINC SENTITS (€€€)

cincsentits.com/en/

Ingredients sourced from all over the
world are lovingly combined at the

SPANISH MEATS

Although pork is the mainstay of meat
dishes, there is plenty of choice for car-
nivores, including brains, sweetbreads,
trotters and other items that have vanished
from other nations' tables. Beef and lamb
are good, and game is excellent, including
pheasant, partridge and wild boar (and
don't ignore the humble rabbit). Try unusual combinations, like duck with pears.

innovative Five Senses restaurant.
Dishes are served as part of a six- or
eight-course tasting menu, and range
from simple grills with a twist to slow-
cooked braises with imaginative
vegetable pairings.

🔲 F6 ✉ Carrer d'Aribau 58 ☎ 93 323 94
90 🕐 Tue–Sat 1.30–3.30, 8.30–11 🚇 Passeig
de Gràcia

CIUDAD CONDAL (€)

This modern tapas restaurant has a
summer terrace. Go for classics such as
Spanish omelette or *tapas bravas*, or
more creative fare like Basque spider
crab or slivers of fried artichokes.

🔲 G6 ✉ Rambla de Catalunya 18 ☎ 93 318
19 97 🕐 Daily 8am–1.30am 🚇 Catalunya

EMBAT (€€)

This cosy place is understated but it's
big among the city's gastro set. Lunches
are good value—you may eat wild
mushroom cannelloni or poached eggs
with chorizo, depending on the season.
At night, a tasting menu may consist of
four tapas-sized courses and a pair of
mouth-watering desserts.

🔲 J5 ✉ Carrer Mallorca 304 ☎ 93 458
08 55 🕐 Mon–Wed 8.30–3.45, Thu–Sat
8.30–3.45, 8.30–11 🚇 Verdaguer

IKIBANA (€€)

ikibana.com

A fashionable restaurant specializing in
Brazilian-Japanese fusion cuisine, Ikibana
also has an outdoor terrace and a
trendy bar. The menu changes accord-
ing to what is in season, but always
includes some creative sushi, fresh seafood dishes and unusual desserts.
There's another branch in the Born.

🔲 H5 ✉ Avinguda del Parallel 148 ☎ 93
424 46 48 🕐 Daily 1.30–4, 8.30–2.30am
🚇 Poble Sec

ROCA MOO (€€€)

hotelomm.com/en/roca-barcelona/roca-moo/
Omm Hotel hosts Michelin-starred Moo,
one of the city's most talked-about restaurants. It serves quirky, molecular
cookery best sampled from the tasting
menu. The dress code is formal.

🔲 G5 ✉ Carrer Rosselló 265 ☎ 93
445 40 00 🕐 Tue–Sat 1.30–4, 8–midnight
🚇 Diagonal

PACO MERALGO (€€)

restaurantpacomeralgo.com/home/
Scandi-style long benches and high
stools adorn this upmarket tapas bar,
where you can enjoy classics such as
oven-baked clams, home-made *empa-
nadillas* (small pies) and more
substantial Mediterranean rice dishes
and stews. The wine list is equally good.

🔲 F5 ✉ Carrer Muntaner 171 ☎ 93
430 90 27 🕐 Daily 1.30–4, 8.30–12.30am
🚇 Diagonal

EL PRINCIPAL (€€)

elprincipaleixample.com
This charming restaurant serves delicious Mediterranean cuisine and has a
shady courtyard where you can eat in
summer. There's also a tapas bar if
you're looking for something lighter.

🔲 J5 ✉ Carrer Provença 286–8 ☎ 93 272
08 45 🕐 Daily 11am–midnight 🚇 Diagonal

SPECIAL TODAY

Many local people make lunch the main
meal of the day and eat relatively frugally
in the evening. One reason for following
their example is to benefit from the bargain
menú del día (fixed-price menu). It is likely
to consist of three courses plus bread and a
drink, which would cost considerably more
if the dishes were selected individually,
particularly in the evening.

Around the central city, there's a clutch of sights that combine Barcelona's history with its present-day preoccupations. Pedralbes gives an insight into the medieval world and grand early-20th-century living, while Tibidabo and Camp Nou represent its modern pleasures.

Torre de
Collserola

Parc d'Atraccions
de Tibidabo

C-16
E-9

N

Parc de
Collserola

B-20

CosmoCaixa

RONDA DE DALT

VIA AUGUSTA

B-20

PASSEIG DE SANT GERVASI

Museu
Monestir
de Pedralbes

B-20

Parc de
Cervantes

CARRER DE BALMES

A-2 E-90

Palau de
Pedralbes

Parc del Turó
del Putget

Parc del
Palau de
Pedralbes

AVINGUDA DIAGONAL

GRAN VIA DE CARLES III

RONDA DEL GENERAL MITRE

VIA AUGUSTA

AVINGUDA DE SARRIÀ

Camp Nou

CARRER DE NUMÀNCIA

Turó
Park

CARRER DE BALMES

CARRER DEL BRASIL

AVINGUDA DIAGONAL

VIA AUGUSTA

CARRER DE BADAL

CARRER DE
BERLÍN

CARRER DE PARÍS

CARRER DE BALMES

L'EIXAM

CARRER DE
TARRAGONA

Parc de
l'Espanya
Industrial

CARRER D'ENTENÇA

CARRER D'ARAGÓ

RAMBLA DE CATALUNYA

PASSEIG DE GRÀCIA

Parc de
l'Alhambra

Parc de
Joan Miró

GRAN VIA DE LES CORTS CATALANES

LAS RAMBLAS

GRAN VIA DE LES
CORTS CATALANES

C-31

PASSEIG DE LA ZONA FRANCA

AVINGUDA DEL PARAL·LEL

EL RAVAL

BARCELONA

VIA LAIETANA

Jardins de Sant
Pau del Camp

BARRI
GÒTIC

Muntanya de
Montjuïc

MONTJUÏC

PORT
VELL

RONDA   LITORAL   B-10

BARCELONETA

Parc de les Heures

B-20

RONDA DE DALT

RONDA DE DALT

Parc de la Guineueta

Parc de la Creueta del Coll

Parc del Turó de la Peira

Parc de Can Drago

Parc Güell

TUNEL DE LA ROVIRA

Parc del Guinardó

TRAVESSERA DE DALT

GRÀCIA

RONDA DEL GUINARDÓ

Parc de les Aigües

AVINGUDA MERIDIANA

Parc Pegaso

SAGRADA FAMÍLIA

MPLE

AVINGUDA DIAGONAL

CARRER D'ARAGÓ

Parc del Clot

VIA DE LES CORTS CATALANES

C-31

Parc de l'Estació del Nord

AVINGUDA MERIDIANA

AVINGUDA DIAGONAL

LA RIBERA

PASSEIG DE PICASSO

Parc de la Ciutadella

CARRER DE LA MARINA

Parc Diagonal Mar

RONDA LITORAL

Parc del Poblenou

Museu Blau

B-10

PORT OLÍMPIC

0 _____ 1 km

0 _____ 1 mile

Museu Monestir de Pedralbes

TOP 25

Only a bus ride away from the bustle of central Barcelona stands one of Europe's best-preserved and most atmospheric medieval monasteries. It also has an intriguing museum of monastic life.

Monastic museum Once a foothill village outside Barcelona, Pedralbes still exudes a rustic atmosphere, with a cobbled street leading steeply upward to the fortified walls of the great monastery. The nuns first came here in the 14th century and have stayed ever since. They moved into a new residence in 1983, and the historic parts of the monastery have become a fascinating museum of monastic life. The building contains works of art, liturgical objects and furniture accumulated over the centuries. The core of the establishment is the Gothic cloister,

three floors high, with elegant columns and capitals. In the middle are palms, orange trees and cypresses; around it are spaces once used for community activities. The simple cells contrast with the grandeur of the refectory with its vaulted ceiling, and you'll see a pharmacy, infirmary, the kitchens and the great cistern. The chapter house has mementos of monastic life, including the funereal urn of Sobirana de Olzet, the first abbess.

The Church of Pedralbes The nuns still worship in the Gothic church next to the monastery and the sounds of their vespers are often heard in the street outside. This is a popular place for locals to tie the knot, and it is said that if the bride brings the nuns a dozen eggs the day before the wedding, it won't rain on the big day.

THE BASICS

➕ C1

✉ Baixada del Monestir 9

☎ 93 256 34 34

🕐 Apr–Sep Tue–Fri 10–5, Sat 10–7, Sun 10–8; Oct–Mar Tue–Fri 10–2, Sat–Sun 10–5

Ⓡ Reina Elisenda

🚌 63, 66, 75, 78, 113, H4

♿ Good

💷 Inexpensive; free Sun after 3pm and all day 1st Sun of month

Camp Nou

TOP
25

The Camp Nou, home of FC Barcelona, is Europe's biggest football stadium

THE BASICS

fcbarcelona.com

🔲 B3

✉ Aristides Maillol, Entrance 14

☎ 902 189 900

🕐 Jul to mid-Sep daily 9–7.30; Nov–Mar Mon–Sat 10–6.30, Sun and bank holidays 10–2.30; rest of year Mon–Sat 9.30–7, Sun 9.30–2.30

🚇 Collblanc

🚌 15, 54, 113, L12

♿ Fair

👋 Expensive

HIGHLIGHTS

● Tour of the stadium
● Players' tunnel
● Collection of cups and trophies
● Videos of match highlights

TIP

● Buy tickets in advance online (tickets.fcbarcelona.com) to avoid queues.

FC Barcelona is one of the richest and most successful football clubs in the world. It has won the Spanish Liga, the Copa del Rey and the European UEFA Champions League ("the continental treble") a record-breaking three times. Its home stadium, the Camp Nou, is the largest in Europe.

More than a club Usually known simply as Barça, the club has worn the distinctive "blaugrana" (blue and maroon) striped shirts since its earliest days. The suppression of Catalan language and traditions under the Franco regime made FC Barcelona a potent symbol of Catalan identity, and Barça's slogan remains "Més que un club ("More than a club"). The 99,000-seat Camp Nou stadium, the home of the club, was originally built in the 1950s thanks in part to its members, who paid their fees early to meet the building costs. The club approved ambitious redevelopment plans in 2016, which will create an eco-friendly stadium with increased capacity.

Camp Nou Experience The museum dedicated to FC Barcelona is the city's third most visited attraction after the Sagrada Família and Park Güell. In the interactive galleries, you can admire the team's collection of cups and trophies, relive moments of glory in the video displays, and take in a vast collection of memorabilia. A tour of the stadium, including the players' tunnel and dressing rooms, remains the undisputed highlight of the visit.

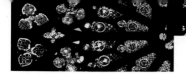

More to See

COSMOCAIXA

cosmocaixa.es

Housed in a splendid *modernista* building at the foot of the Tibidabo heights, this Museum of Science is the finest of its kind in Spain. Many of the exhibits and displays encourage participation, and it is loved by children.

➕ G1 ✉ Carrer de Isaac Newton 26 ☎ 93 212 60 50 🕐 Tue–Sun 10–8 🍴 Café 🚇 Tibidabo, then Tramvia Blau ♿ Good 💰 Inexpensive

MUSEU BLAU

museuciencies.cat

Museu Blau is the main seat of Barcelona's Museum of Natural History (Museu de Ciències Naturals). It's a fantastic, high-tech museum housed in a stunning, cobalt-blue building. There are interactive exhibits in the Planet Life exhibition, rare gemstones and a huge whale skeleton suspended over the entrance. Outside, there are open spaces and a playground where kids can let off steam.

➕ See map ▷ 101 ✉ Rambla Prim 1 🕐 Mar–Sep Tue–Sat 10–7, Sun 10–8; Oct–Feb Tue–Fri 10–6, Sat 10–7, Sun 10–8 🚇 El Maresme/Fòrum ♿ Good 💰 Moderate

PALAU DE PEDRALBES

The Palau de Pedralbes was donated to the Spanish monarchs by the Güell family in the 1920s, when it was expanded to accommodate its new royal owners. Eusebi Güell, a wealthy industrialist, was Gaudí's most important benefactor, and Gaudí was responsible for the charming fountain in the gardens, as well as the magnificent gates bearing a wrought-iron dragon, which adorn the gatehouse at the back of the property. The palace is not currently open to the public, but its glorious gardens are perfect for a stroll or a picnic, and provide a charming backdrop for summer concerts held as part of the annual Pedralbes Festival (end-June/early July).

➕ C2 ✉ Diagonal 686 🕐 Daily 10–dusk 🚇 Palau Reial 🚌 60, 63, 75, 78, 113, H4 ♿ Fair 💰 Access to gardens free

The CosmoCaixa houses Barcelona's Museum of Science

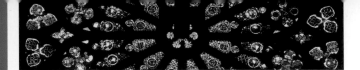

PARC D'ATRACCIONS DE TIBIDABO

tibidabo.cat

Spectacularly set atop Tibidabo mountain, this delightfully old-fashioned theme park retains traditional attractions such as the hall of mirrors, the red monoplane (1922) and the Haunted Castle (1955). You'll also find a couple of small roller coasters and a log flume, all with stunning views over the whole city.
✚ See map ▷ 100 ✉ Plaça del Tibidabo ☎ 93 211 79 42 ⏰ Opening hours change weekly; check website for times 🚆 FGC Tibidabo then Tramvia Blau and funicular to park 🎟 Tibidabo: expensive

PARC DE COLLSEROLA

parcdecollserola.net

Many bring their bikes to this rural park north of the city and ride along the Carretera de les Aigües, a route that skirts the western flank of Tibidabo and offers a spectacular panorama of the entire city. There are lots of well-posted walking tracks, on which you may spot some of the local wildlife, including the famous *jabalí* (wild boar). The park contains the Museu Casa Verdaguer, former home of Catalonia's most revered poet. The park's information centre can supply maps and advice.
✚ See map ▷ 100 ✉ Information centre: Carretera de Vallvidrera a Sant Cugat ☎ Information centre 93 280 35 52; museum 93 204 78 05 ⏰ Information centre daily 9.30–3; museum Sat, Sun and hols 10–2 🍴 Bar/restaurant 🚆 Baixador de Vallvidrera (FGC) then short walk 🎟 Museum: free

TORRE DE COLLSEROLA

torredecollserola.com

This futuristic landmark on the hills of Collserola was built as a communications tower for the 1992 Olympic Games and is the highest point in the city. Visitors can ride an elevator to a viewing platform.
✚ See map ▷ 100 ✉ Carretera de Vallvidrera al Tibidabo s/n ☎ 93 211 79 42 ⏰ Jul–Aug Wed–Sat noon–11; times vary other months 🚆 Peu de Funicular (FGC) then funicular and bus 11 🎟 Moderate; combined ticket with Tibidabo available

All the fun of the fair at Tibidabo

A view from Tibidabo toward the Torre de Collserola

Barcelona's popularity means that there's plenty of choice for places to stay, whatever your budget. Options range from boutique guest houses to *modernista* classics and state-of-the-art hotels.

Introduction

All accommodation in Catalonia is officially regulated by the Generalitat, the regional government, and is broken down into two main categories, hotels and *hostals*.

What's the Difference?

Hotels are denoted by (H) and rated on a scale of one to five stars. All rooms must have a private bathroom to qualify as a hotel, and the number of stars is determined by the amenities provided. Simpler hotels rarely have restaurants or provide breakfast. In the past five years Barcelona has seen an explosion of smart urban hotels. Facilities such as rooftop pools, stylish lobbies and designer features are becoming more and more common. *Hostals* (HS) sometimes classify themselves as *fondes*, *pensións* or *residències*. They're rated on a scale of one to three stars and are normally less expensive than hotels. Many have been renovated over the past 15 years or so and will have some rooms with bathrooms. *Hostals* tend to be family-run; very few have restaurants and many don't serve breakfast.

Reservations

Despite the plethora of new accommodations, finding a room in Barcelona can be difficult, especially during major trade events, so it pays to book as far ahead as you can to secure something central. If you haven't reserved a room in advance, the tourist offices in the Plaça de Catalunya and the Plaça de Sant Jaume have hotel reservation desks where you will usually be able to find something. They charge a deposit against the cost of the room.

WHERE TO STAY

If you want to be in the heart of the action, reserve accommodation around the Ramblas or in the Barri Gòtic, where there's a huge choice, including budget options. The quieter Eixample, too, is well endowed with hotels, and is generally safer than downtown. Nicest of all are either the classy Ribera, or Gràcia, with its laid-back, intimate atmosphere, though hotels in these areas are scarce.

Budget Hotels

PRICES
Expect to pay between €60 and €90 for a budget hotel

B-HOTEL
b-hotel.com

A great-value option next to the Plaça d'Espanya, this has a fabulous rooftop plunge pool, contemporary rooms and a small spa. All this is rounded off with excellent service.

✛ D6 ✉ Gran Via 389–391 ☎ 93 552 95 00 🚇 Espanya

CASA GRÀCIA
casagraciabcn.com

Perfectly located overlooking the swanky Passeig de Gràcia, just steps from La Pedrera and the Casa Batlló, this attractive guest house offers simple, stylish rooms, a huge shared kitchen, a cosy living room with comfy armchairs, and a spacious terrace where you can soak up the sun.

✛ H6 ✉ Passeig de Gràcia 116 ☎ 93 187 44 97 🚇 Diagonal

CHIC & BASIC TALLERS
chicandbasic.com

The name says it all for this boutique *hostal*. Rooms are a bit small, but are decked out in minimalist decor and equipped with extras such as flat-screen TVs and iPod docks.

✛ G7 ✉ Carrer Tallers 82 ☎ 93 342 66 66 🚇 Universitat

HOSTAL GIRONA
hostalgirona.com

The reception area, with its antique furniture and Persian rugs, gives a foretaste of the quality of this superb *hostal*. Rooms are bright and simple, with big windows and tiled floors; some have private bathrooms, and many have balconies overlooking Carrer Girona or the inner courtyard.

✛ H7 ✉ Carrer de Girona 24 ☎ 93 265 02 59 🚇 Urquinaona

HOSTAL ORLEANS
hostalorleans.com

Between Barceloneta's beach and the trendy El Born district, you couldn't do much better on a budget. Most rooms have been refurbished and are comfortable with en suites. Some look out onto a busy thoroughfare, so if noise is an issue ask for an interior room.

✛ H8 ✉ Avinguda Marqués de Argentera 13 ☎ 93 319 73 82 🚇 Barceloneta

HOTEL CURIOUS
hotelcurious.com

This renovated, family-run *hostal* is located in the heart of the Raval, close to Las Ramblas. Hardwood floors and chocolate, grape and cream decor, with splashes of photographic wall art sum up the look; free WiFi and a hearty buffet breakfast are a plus. Rooms are not overly large, but given the location, you probably won't be spending much time inside.

✛ G7 ✉ Carrer del Carme 25 ☎ 93 301 44 84 🚇 Liceu

SELF-CATERING
Barcelona has hundreds of self-catering holiday apartments available for short-term rent. Unless you are in Barcelona already, the best place to reserve self-catering accommodations is on the internet. Reputable agencies include oh-barcelona. com and selfcateringholidays.com. Check out the location from an independent source such as tmb.net and ask about extra costs such as cleaning.

Mid-Range Hotels

BANYS ORIENTALS

hotelbanysorientals.com

Situated on one of the Born's busiest streets, this friendly hotel lives up to the area's style credentials without skimping on the service. It offers larger suites in an annexe in a nearby building.

✚ H8 ✉ Carr de Argentería 37 ☎ 93 268 84 60 🚇 Jaume 1

BARCELÓ RAVAL

barceloraval.com

A striking cylindrical building, where the rooms are spacious and afford splendid views, boasts a "James Bond meets Barbarella" decor, with 70s-inspired furniture and bold colour. The rooftop terrace is small, but redeemed by the fact that you can walk all the way around it for a 360-degree view of the city's skyline from 360 degrees. Downstairs, the B-Lounge hosts DJs on the weekends, drawing an international crowd.

✚ F7 ✉ Rambla del Raval 17-21 ☎ 93 320 14 90 🚇 Drassanes

GAUDÍ

hotelgaudi.es

There are Gaudi-esque touches throughout this modern hotel, starting with a lovely reproduction fountain in the entrance foyer. The rooms are comfortable, if a little dark on the lower floors, but the hotel has an enviable location opposite the Palau Güell—from the rooftop sun terrace guests can enjoy exclusive views of the Palau's varied chimneypots.

✚ G8 ✉ Carrer Nou de la Rambla 12 ☎ 93 317 90 32 🚇 Drassanes

HOTEL 54

hotel54barceloneta.com

The ultra-urban Hotel 54 is one of only a few hotels in Barceloneta, so if staying a stone's throw from the beach in stylish surroundings appeals then look no farther. Rooms are small, but with all the designer trappings and fabulous views of the port. The rooftop bar and terrace is a great place to chill out.

✚ H9 ✉ Passeig de Joan de Borbo 54 ☎ 93 225 00 54 🚇 Barceloneta

HOTEL BALMES

hotelbalmes.com

A small outdoor pool in a pretty rear garden sets this great-value, four-star hotel apart, and can prove a godsend in the hot summer months. Close to the shopping hub of Passeig de Gràcia, the Balmes' rooms, while not overly spacious, are stylish and comfortable and the hotel also offers a sauna.

✚ G5 ✉ Carrer Mallorca 216 ☎ 93 445 65 00 🚇 Diagonal

HOTEL CONSTANZA

hotelconstanza.com

Representing great value for money, this elegant, Japanese-inspired boutique hotel is brilliantly situated for shopping and sights. It has a fabulous roof terrace where you can lounge in comfort.

✚ H6 ✉ Carrer del Bruc 33 ☎ 93 270 19 10 🚇 Urquinaona

HOTEL JAZZ

hoteljazz.com

A chic, modern hotel with an unbeatably central location on one of the city's main shopping streets, this has bright, soundproofed rooms, a fantastic roof terrace with a plunge pool and friendly, helpful staff.

🔒 G7 ✉ Carrer Pelai 3 ☎ 93 552 96 96 🚇 Catalunya

HOTEL SANT AUGUSTÍ

hotelsa.com

This old monastery building on a tree-shaded Raval square was converted to a hotel in 1840, making it the oldest in Barcelona. It's kept up with the times and its handsome, high-ceilinged rooms are well-equipped and comfortable. Off the greenery-filled, elegant marble lobby, there's a relaxing bar and restaurant.

🔒 G7 ✉ Plaça de Sant Agustí 3 ☎ 93 318 16 58 🚇 Liceu

HOTEL SOHO

hotelsohobarcelona.com

This 54-room hotel wears its "designer" stripes loud and proud, but unlike others in its genre, the mod-con trappings will enhance your stay rather than merely decorate it. There's a stunning terrace with a rooftop plunge pool, where you can cool off after a day's sightseeing. Ask for a rear room: these are quieter and have a spacious terrace overlooking a courtyard.

🔒 F6 ✉ Gran Via de les Corts Catalanes 543–545 ☎ 93 552 96 10 🚇 Urgell

HUSA ORIENTE

husa.es

At the somewhat seedy lower end of the Ramblas, the mid-19th-century Oriente has long since ceased to be *the* place to stay in Barcelona, but its ornate public spaces and only slightly less alluring 142 rooms continue to attract customers who like lodgings with some character. Previous guests include Hans Christian Andersen and Errol Flynn.

🔒 G8 ✉ La Rambla 45 ☎ 93 302 25 58 🚇 Liceu, Drassanes

MARKET HOTEL

markethotel.com.es

Above a smart restaurant of the same name, this hotel offers stylish comfort that is normally associated with much more expensive hotels. Rooms boast hardwood floors, oriental Zen-inspired furniture, quality linen and abstract art. There's also a restaurant and a comfortable cocktail lounge with a terrace.

🔒 E7 ✉ Carrer del Comte Borrell 68 ☎ 93 325 12 05 🚇 Sant Antoni

MUSIK BOUTIQUE HOTEL

musikboutiquehotel.com

Tucked away near the magnificent Palau de la Música, this boutique hotel provides chic, modern rooms behind a handsome 18th-century facade. The air-conditioned and soundproofed guest rooms are elegantly decorated and come with extras like iPod docks and WiFi; some boast private balconies.

🔒 H7 ✉ Carrer Sant Pere Més Baix 62 ☎ 93 222 55 44 🚇 Urquinaona

PRAKTIK GARDEN

praktikhotels.com

A 19th-century building in the Eixample has been made into a chilled, minimalist, urban hotel while still keeping original features such as colourful mosaic flooring and florid ceiling mouldings. There's a plant-filled terrace where you can relax after a day's sightseeing.

🔒 H6 ✉ Carrer de Diputació 325 ☎ 93 467 52 79 🚇 Girona, Tetuan

Luxury Hotels

PRICES

Expect to pay between €150 and €350 for a luxury hotel

CASA FUSTER

hotelcasafuster.com

Designed in 1911, this magnificent building has undergone a restoration that unites sleek modern design with the glory of the past. The opulent rooms retain period features but offer cutting-edge technology and superb comfort.
➕ G5 ✉ Passeig de Gràcia 132 ☎ 93 255 30 00 🚇 Diagonal

GRAND HOTEL CENTRAL

grandhotelcentral.com

With a reputation for having the best rooftop terrace in the city, this smooth-as-silk hotel is a popular choice with style setters. The spacious rooms are decorated in calming earth tones.
➕ H7 ✉ Vía Laietana 30 ☎ 93 295 79 00 🚇 Jaume I

HOTEL 1898

hotel1898.com

This attractive hotel has an art deco theme, with palms, patterned floors and ship's-cabin style in the 169 rooms. It has a spa and rooftop pool and is the only luxury option right on Las Ramblas.
➕ G7 ✉ Las Ramblas 109 ☎ 93 552 95 52 🚇 Catalunya

HOTEL DUQUESA DE CARDONA

hduquesadecardona.com

This romantic hotel occupies a tastefully restored 16th-century building, furnished with mainly natural materials. The roof terrace has a small but welcome swimming pool.
➕ G8 ✉ Passeig de Colom 12 ☎ 93 268 90 90 🚇 Drassanes

HOTEL NERI

hotelneri.com

This handsome palace deep in the Gothic quarter has been stunningly converted into a luxurious boutique hotel. It boasts sumptuous, oriental interiors making good use of natural stone, combining mod cons and smooth comfort.
➕ G7 ✉ Carrer Sant Sever 5 ☎ 93 304 06 55 🚇 Jaume 1

HOTEL PULITZER

hotelpulitzer.es

The Pulitzer stands just behind the Plaça Catalunya, providing stylish hotel comfort in the city's main hub. The rooms and public areas contain an impressive collection of antiques and abstract art, and the Japanese-style bathrooms and rooftop terrace are a real draw.
➕ G7 ✉ Carrer Bergara 8 ☎ 93 481 67 67 🚇 Catalunya

W BARCELONA

starwoodhotels.com

Jutting out from the southern tip of Barceloneta beach, the soaring, sail-shaped W is designed to impress. The spacious rooms enjoy glorious coastal views, while a top-floor bar and mezzanine-level wet deck provide a resort feel.
➕ Off map ✉ Plaça de la Rosa dels Vents 1 ☎ 93 295 28 00 🚌 64

SLEEPLESS CITY

Beware of noise. Barcelona is not a quiet city, and many of its citizens never seem to go to bed. A room on the Ramblas may have a wonderful view, but without super-efficient double-glazing, undisturbed slumber cannot be guaranteed. Accommodation overlooking an unglamorous nearby skylight may be less picturesque, but could possibly prove a wiser choice.

Need to Know

Use this section to familiarize yourself with travel to and within Barcelona. The Essential Facts will give you insider knowledge of the city. You'll also find a few basic language tips.

Planning Ahead

When to Go

Barcelona has no off-season—there is always something to see and do. However, May to June and mid-September to mid-November are ideal visiting times, with perfect temperatures and not too many visitors. Summer can be very hot, and you'll have to contend with the crowds.

TIME

Spain is 6 hours ahead of New York City, 9 hours ahead of Los Angeles, and 1 hour ahead of the UK.

AVERAGE DAILY MAXIMUM TEMPERATURES

JAN	FEB	MAR	APR	MAY	JUN	JUL	AUG	SEP	OCT	NOV	DEC
57°F	59°F	63°F	66°F	72°F	77°F	84°F	84°F	81°F	73°F	64°F	59°F
14°C	15°C	17°C	19°C	22°C	25°C	29°C	29°C	27°C	23°C	18°C	15°C

Spring (March to May) is a good time to visit: pleasantly warm though sometimes cloudy.
Summer (June to September) is the hottest season with very high temperatures in July and August.
Autumn (October to November) is normally Barcelona's wettest season, with heavy rain and thunderstorms as summer heat abates.
Winter (December to February) brings rain up to Christmas, followed by cooler, drier weather, though temperatures are rarely much below 10°C (50°F).

WHAT'S ON

January *Three Kings* (6 Jan): The kings arrive by boat and shower children with sweets.
February/March *Carnestoltes:* Boisterous pre-Lenten carnival celebrations include a major costumed procession and the symbolic burial of a sardine. Sitges' carnival is particularly festive.
Easter Celebrated in style in the outer districts with a southern Spanish population.
April *St. Jordi (St.George's Day,* 23 Apr): The festival of Catalonia's patron saint is marked by lovers' gifts:

roses for the woman, a book for the man. There are open-air book fairs and impressive floral displays.
June/July *Sant Joan* (23–24 Jun): An excuse for mass partying and for locals to set off fireworks from their balconies or down on the beach.
Festival del Grec (Jun–Aug): A festival of music, plays and dance.
August *Festa Major de Gràcia:* A week of street celebrations in the city's most vibrant suburb, village-like Gràcia.
September *Diada de Catalunya* (11 Sep): Flags

wave on the Catalan National Day, and political demonstrations are likely.
Festas de la Mercè (19–25 Sep): The four-day festival celebrating the city's patron saint, Our Lady of Mercy, is Barcelona's biggest. Music, plays, *sardana* dancing, parades, fireworks and spectacles featuring giants, dragons and *castellers* (human towers) all occur.
December *The Christmas Season:* Preparations include a grand manger scene in Plaça de Sant Jaume (▷ 51) and a market in front of the cathedral.

Barcelona Online

barcelonaturisme.com
Barcelona's official tourist website has a wealth of information on every aspect of the city. In English, and regularly updated, it's the obvious place to research your trip. You can buy tickets to most sights and attractions online.

spain.info
The main Spanish tourist board site is loaded with details about both Barcelona and its local environs.

barcelona-metropolitan.com
The city's premier English-language magazine gives the low-down on what's on and what's new in the bar, restaurant and nightclub scene, as well as inspiration for days out of town and a handy classified section for apartments and jobs.

barcelonahotels.es
Run by Barcelona's hotelier association, this site has a good choice of mid-range, mid-price hotels with online booking.

bcn.cat
This site, in English, is run by Barcelona's city council and is primarily aimed at locals. There is an excellent tourism section, with details of opening times, exhibitions and more.

tmb.cat
All you need to know about fares, routes and the timetables of Barcelona's bus and metro systems.

fcbarcelona.com
Even if you're not a football fan, this official site gives an insight into the passions the team evokes.

barcelona.lecool.com
A carefully selected roundup of hip cultural and music events for the coming week.

TRAVEL SITES

fodors.com
A complete travel-planning site. You can research prices and weather; book air tickets, cars and rooms; ask questions (and get answers) from fellow travellers; and find links to other sites.

renfe.com
The official site of Spanish National Railways.

wunderground.com
Good weather forecasting, updated three times daily.

INTERNET CONNECTION

Barcelona is one of the easiest European cities in which to go online. More and more hotels are offering WiFi options as are many bars and cafés (look for the WiFi symbol). *Locutorios* are cheap call venues, with phone booths that let you call home at a less expensive rate than either the hotels or public phone booths. A high percentage of these also have internet facilities. They are mostly found in the Raval, Barri Gòtic and Barceloneta districts. Free hotspots in the city include Sants train station and Santa Caterina market—though connection is limited to an hour. See bcn.cat/barcelonawifi/en for a full list of hotspots.

Getting There

INSURANCE

US citizens should check their insurance coverage and buy a supplementary policy as needed. EU nationals receive medical treatment on production of the free European emergency health card (EHIC). You should obtain this before leaving home. Full health and travel insurance is still advised.

In case of emergency, go to the casualty department of any of the major hospitals; Hospital Clínic (Villaroel 170, tel 93 227 54 00, 🚇 Hospital Clínic) and Hospital del Mar (Passeig Marítim, tel 93 248 30 00, 🚇 Ciutadella Vila Olímpica) are the most central.

BARCELONA AIRPORT

Barcelona airport consists of two terminals; T1 and T2. Over 50 companies operate from T1, including Star Alliance, British Airways, Iberia and the low-cost Spanish carrier Vueling. More airlines are being added, so check which terminal your flight leaves from. A bus shuttle runs between TI and T2 and the airport's train station (at T2); the journey takes 10 minutes. Both terminals offer the same facilities.

AIRPORTS

Barcelona's modern airport is spread over two terminals at El Prat de Llobregat. T1 services most international carriers, while T2 services smaller companies. Connections to both are good, though vary from one to the other; make sure you know which terminal you need before setting off.

FROM BARCELONA AIRPORT (EL PRAT)

Barcelona's airport (tel 902 40 47 04; aena.es) is well served by city links.

The convenient Aerobus service connects both T1 and T2 with Plaça de Catalunya via Plaça d'Espanya and Gran Via de les Corts Catalanes (and Sants station for travel to the airport). The A1 bus runs to T1 and the A2 bus to T2: be sure to catch the right one. The A1 bus runs from 5am to 12.30am and the A2 bus from 5.35am to 1.05am: services operate every 5 to 10 minutes, and the journey takes about 30 minutes.

Trains (line R2 Nord) operate from Passeig de Gràcia and Sants station to the airport, and run every 30 minutes from 5.13am to 11.14pm. Tickets are €2.50 one way and the T10 ticket is also valid. Taxis are available outside the airport terminals; the journey takes about 20–30 minutes, depending on traffic, and costs about €25–€30.

ARRIVING BY TRAIN

Barcelona is connected to all major cities within Spain and a number of destinations in Europe,

namely Paris, Geneva, Zürich and Milan. These trains arrive and depart at Sants Estació, the city's main station, which also has regular bus and metro services to central Barcelona and elsewhere. A few regional trains leave from the stations Estació de França in the old town (predominantly southbound) and from Passeig de Gràcia in the new town (mainly northbound).

ARRIVING BY BUS
Direct bus services operate from several European countries. The bus station is Estació d'Autobus Barcelona Nord, next to Arc de Triomf rail and metro station, tel 902 26 06 06; barcelonanord.cat.

ARRIVING BY CAR
Barcelona is connected by the AP7 toll *autopista* to the French frontier and motorway network at La Jonquera (144km/90 miles northeast). Toulouse is 368km (245 miles) north via N152, the French frontier at Puigcerdà and RN20. Motorway access to the rest of Spain is via *autopista* AP2 and AP7. However, driving is not recommended in Barcelona itself; traffic is heavy and can be intimidating; most of the city streets are part of what can be a bewildering one-way system and parking is at a premium, with virtually no on-street parking for visitors in the downtown area. If you are driving, you could leave your car in one of the long-term airport parking areas.

ARRIVING BY SEA
Car ferry services from Britain to Spain are operated by Brittany Ferries (tel 0330 159 7000, Plymouth–Santander, Portsmouth–Santander and Portsmouth–Bilbao). Ferries and cruise ships arrive at Barcelona's Port Terminal at the southern end of Las Ramblas. Ferries connect Rome and Genova in Italy and the Balearic Islands of Ibiza, Mallorca and Menorca. For the latter, the largest operator is Trasmediterránea, tel 902 45 46 45; trasmediterranea.es.

ENTRY REQUIREMENTS

In June 2007, the Spanish government introduced the API (Advanced Passenger Information) rule. It means all travellers need to provide the airline with the details on the photo page of their passport before departure. Many carriers have introduced a facility on their website that lets you do this online.

NEED TO KNOW GETTING THERE

Getting Around

Although Barcelona is a walker's city *par excellence*, at some point you will want to use the first-rate bus and metro (subway) system, which is supplemented by funiculars, a limited tramline and the historic Tramvia Blau, which climbs to the base of Tibidabo. Buses, the metro and the suburban railway, FGC, are fully integrated and tickets can be used on any of them in any combination. Pick up a map of the network from a tourist information point or one of the TMB offices; these are in the metro stations at Plaça de la Universitat, Barcelona-Sants and Sagrada Família and Sagrera.
● For information, call 902 07 50 27.

TICKETS
One-way tickets are available, but it makes sense to pay for multiple journeys using one of several types of *targeta* (travelcard):
● *Targeta* 10 (or T10) is valid for 10 trips by metro (not to airport), FGC or bus.
● *Targeta* T-Mes is valid for unlimited trips within 30 days by metro (including to the airport), FGC or bus.
● You must cancel one unit of a *targeta* per journey undertaken by inserting it into the automatic machine at the entrance to a station or aboard a bus. Changing from metro or FGC to bus or vice versa within 1 hour is one trip.
● *Targetas* are available only from metro stations; most are operated by vending machine.
● *Hola BCN* is a travelcard available for 2, 3, 4 or 5 days. It offers unlimited use of public transport (including metro to the airport). Buy it from TMB offices or online.

METRO
There are 11 metro lines, identified by number and colour. Direction is indicated by the name of the station at the end of the line.
● The network covers most parts of the city and is being extended (open Mon–Thu and Sun 5am–midnight, Fri and the evening before a public holiday 5am–2am, Sat 24 hours).

TRAINS
● Many mainline trains run beneath the city, stopping at the underground stations at Passeig de Gràcia and Plaça de Catalunya.
● The number for national rail enquiries is 91 232 03 20

BUSES
Buses run 6.30am–10pm, though routes vary. A free map detailing all bus services is available from TMB's information points. As well as one-way tickets, several types of *targeta* (travelcard) can be used on the metro and buses.
● *Targetas* can be bought only at metro stations, not onboard buses.
● More information (including frequency of service) is given on the panels at bus stops.
● There is a night service, the *Nitbus*, with routes around Plaça de Catalunya.
● Useful tourist routes include numbers 22 (Plaça de Catalunya–Gràcia–Tramvia Blau) and 24 (Plaça de Catalunya–Gràcia–Park Güell).

TAXIS
● Black-and-yellow taxis can easily be hailed on the street when displaying a green light and the sign Lliure/Libre (free). There are large taxi stands at the northern end of Las Ramblas (opposite Plaça Catalunya) and at the southern end opposite the Columbus monument.
● Fares are not expensive, but a series of supplements—for luggage, airport runs (minimum fare €20) and past-midnight rides—can bump up the fare.

ORGANIZED SIGHTSEEING
The best buy in city sightseeing is the Bus Turístic, which has three routes—one running north of the city (green), one south and west (red) and one eastward (blue). One- and two-day tickets entitle you to discounts on many sights. Tickets are sold at the Tourist Information Centre in Plaça Catalunya and TMB offices. Barcelona City Tour (tel 93 317 64 54) offers the same service from a red double-decker bus.

TAXI CONTACTS
If you need to call a taxi, try these reputable services:
Barna Taxi
✉ 93 357 77 55
Servi Taxi
✉ 93 330 03 00
Radio Taxi
✉ 902 222 111
Taxi Class Rent
✉ 93 307 07 07

TOURIST INFORMATION
✚ G7 ✉ Plaça Catalunya s/n ◷ Daily 9–9

✚ D5 ✉ Estació de Sants ◷ Mon–Fri 8–8, Sat–Sun 8–2 (until 8 in summer)

✚ G8 ✉ Carrer Ciutat 2 (Ajuntament) ◷ Mon–Fri 9–8, Sat 10–8, Sun 10–2

✚ G7 ✉ Las Ramblas 115 ◷ Daily 9–9

✚ Off map ✉ El Prat airport terminals T1 and T2 ◷ Daily 9–9

Tourist Info phone line:
☎ 93 285 38 34

Essential Facts

TRAVELLER BEWARE

Be aware that, in certain areas of the city, petty crime rates are very high. Often thefts will occur using diversionary tactics to distract tourists' attention. The Raval area is particularly notorious after dark. Follow commonsense rules, such as carrying little cash and few credit cards, don't wear expensive jewellery, and leave passports and tickets in the hotel. If you are unfortunate enough to be a victim, you must report the theft to the police and be issued with a crime report in order to claim on your insurance.

USEFUL PHONE NUMBERS

● Police, fire and ambulance ☎ 112
● Nacional Police ☎ 091
● Local police ☎ 092
● General city information ☎ 010
● To report a crime ☎ 902 102 112 (English-speaking operators 9am–9pm)

CUSTOMS REGULATIONS

● The limits for non-EU visitors are 200 cigarettes or 50 cigars, or 250g of tobacco; 1 litre of spirits (over 22 per cent) or 2 litres of fortified wine, 2 litres of still wine; 50g of perfume. The guidelines for EU residents (for personal use) are 800 cigarettes, or 200 cigars, or 1kg tobacco; 10 litres of spirits (over 22 per cent), 20 litres of aperitifs, or 90 litres of wine, of which 60 can be sparkling, or 110 litres of beer.
● Visitors under 17 are not entitled to the tobacco and alcohol allowances.

ELECTRICITY

● The standard current is 220/225 volts AC (sometimes 110/125 volts AC).
● Plugs are of round two-pin type. US visitors require an adaptor and a transformer.

OPENING HOURS

● Banks: Mon–Fri 8.30–2.
● Shops: Mon–Sat 9 or 10–1.30, 4.30–8 (hours vary). Larger shops/department stores may open all day. Some Sunday opening.
● Some small museums shut for lunch, close early on Sunday and are shut all day Monday.
● Pharmacies (*farmàcies*) offer a wider range of treatments and medicines than in many countries. Opening hours: Mon–Sat 9–1.30, 4.30–8 (some close on Saturday afternoons).

HEALTH

● If you need a doctor, ask at your hotel as a first step. If you do not have private insurance you will only be entitled to see a doctor working within the Spanish State Health Service.
● Pharmacies are marked by a flashing green cross and operate a rota system, so there is at least one open in every neighbourhood 24 hours a day. Farmàcia Alvarez, Passeig de Gràcia 26 and Farmàcia Clapés, La Rambla 98 are always open 24/7.

MONEY

● Credit cards are widely accepted and can be used in hotels, restaurants and shops and in the automatic ticketing machines for the metro and RENFE (Spanish rail) lines.

● ATMs (*cajeros*) are found all over the city, with operating instructions in several languages, including English.

TOURIST CARDS AND SERVICES

Various *targetas* (cards) offering great discounts on attractions are available at tourist information offices (▷ 119). You can also buy them at a discount online through barcelonacard.org.

● The Barcelona Card (cost €45–€60, valid for 72, 96 or 120 hours) gives unlimited access to public transport and discounts at more than 100 museums restaurants and shops.

● Barcelona Card Express (cost €18, valid for 48 hours) gives unlimited access to public transport and discounts at more than 100 attractions.

● The Articket allows entry to six of the city's major museums and galleries, including MACBA, the Fundació Joan Miró, Museu Picasso and the Museu Nacional d'Art de Catalunya; cost €30.

● Barcelona Turisme's walking tours are organized around themes, and cost approx €9–€22.

● Barcelona Turisme is not the only place where tourists can gather information. The Centre d'Informació de la Virreina (Las Ramblas 99, tel 93 301 7775) has brochures and information on the city's fiestas and cultural events, while the Palau Robert (Passeig de Gràcia 107, tel 93 238 4000) has information on out-of-town destinations within Catalonia.

CURRENCY

The euro is the official currency of Spain. Notes come in denominations of 5, 10, 20, 50, 100, 200 and 500 euros and coins in denominations of 1, 2, 5, 10, 20 and 50 cents, and 1 and 2 euros.

ETIQUETTE

● It's normal to wish people *bon día*. Friends exchange kisses on both cheeks.

● Expect to find unabashed smokers in public places.

● Do not wear shorts or short skirts in churches.

CONSULATES

Canada	✉ Plaça de Catalunya 9	☎ 93 270 36 14
Ireland	✉ Gran Via Carles III 94	☎ 93 491 50 21
Portugal	✉ Ronda San Pedro 7	☎ 93 318 81 50
United Kingdom	✉ Diagonal 477	☎ 90 210 95 36
United States	✉ Passeig Reina Elisenda 23	☎ 93 280 22 27

CHILDREN

● Children are welcome everywhere, but the standard and range of child-specific facilities do not match those available in the UK or US.

● Mother and baby-changing and feeding facilities are rare.

● Hotels will generally be happy to put an extra bed and/or cot in your room for an additional charge.

● Public transport is free for children under 4, but access to the metro with pushchairs (strollers) can be difficult.

● There are no menus specifically for kids, but most restaurants will happily serve children's portions.

● You will find children's play areas in parks and squares all over the city.

● Barcelona's beaches are clean, with play areas, showers and kiosks.

● The tourist board keeps a list of child-minding services.

● You can hire a stroller from Baby Travelling (babytravelling.com).

TELEPHONES

● Since most people now have mobile phones, public phones have all but disappeared in Barcelona.

● For the national operator, call 1009.

● For the international operator from within Spain, call 1409; from elsewhere, 1408.

● For directory enquiries, call 11822; for international enquiries, 11825.

● You must dial Barcelona's code (93), even within Barcelona.

● To phone the US from Spain, prefix the code and number with 001.

● To phone the UK from Spain, dial 00 44, then drop the first zero from the area code.

POST OFFICES

● Main post office (Correu Central) is at Plaça Antoni López, tel 93 486 80 50, open Mon–Fri 8.30am–9.30pm, Sat 8.30–2

● Other post offices are at Aragó 282, Ronda Universitat 23 and Carrer València 231.

● Stamps are sold at paper shops and tobacconists.

● Mailboxes are yellow.

NEWSPAPERS

● International papers are sold at newsstands on the Rambla and Passeig de Gràcia.

● The English-language monthly *Barcelona Metropolitan*, launched in 1996, has some listings and is free.

● The main current events periodical is the weekly *Time Out*.

● *Guía del Ocio* is also sold but is less widely available.

● The Friday edition of *La Vanguardia* contains a supplement *Què Fem?* which is full of listings.

Language

Catalan now enjoys equal status to Castilian Spanish in Barcelona and Catalonia, and must not be thought of as a dialect. Street signs and official communications are now exclusively in Catalan, but virtually everyone understands Castilian Spanish. Most people in the tourist industry speak some English and French. Any effort to speak Spanish or (especially) Catalan will be welcomed.

SOME WORDS TO LOOK OUT FOR

Spanish/Catalan

buenos días/bon dia	good morning
buenas tardes/ bona tarda	good evening
buenas noches/ bona nit	good night
hola/hola	hello
adiós/adéu	goodbye
gracias/gràcies	thank you
perdóne/perdoni	excuse me
de nada/de res	you're welcome
por favor/si us plau	please
si, no/sí, no	yes, no
abierto/obert	open
cerrado/tancat	closed
iglesia/església	church
palacio/palau	palace
museo/museu	museum
calle/carrer	street
aseos, servicios/ lavabo	restroom, toilet
donde/on	where
cuando/quan	when
lunes/dilluns	Monday
martes/dimarts	Tuesday
miércoles/dimecres	Wednesday
jueves/dijous	Thursday
viernes/divendres	Friday
sábado/dissabte	Saturday
domingo/diumenge	Sunday

CALLE OR CARRER

Barcelona's bilingualism needs to be understood when getting around. Both the Spanish *Calle* and Catalan *Carrer* are used to mean "street" though this is mainly dropped in everyday conversation, thus Carrer or Calle de Pau Claris simply becomes "Pau Claris". Although by law all nomenclature must be in Catalan, people still use Spanish versions—compare Comerç (Catalan) to Comercio (Spanish)—though this rarely causes more than a moment of confusion.

NUMBERS

Spanish/Catalan

un, dos/ uno/una, dos	1, 2
tres, cuatro/ tres, quatre	3, 4
cinco, seis/ cinc, sis	5, 6
siete, ocho/ set, vuit	7, 8
nueve, diez/ nou, deu	9, 10
cien/cent	100

Timeline

BEFORE 1000

Barcelona's origins date back to 27BC–AD14, when the Romans founded Barcino during the reign of Emperor Augustus.

City walls were built in the late 3rd/early 4th century, as a result of attacks by Franks and Alemanni.

A Visigothic invasion in AD415 saw the establishment of the Kingdom of Tolosa, the predecessor of Catalonia.

Arabs invaded in 717 and the city became Barjelunah. In 876 the Franks gained control. Catalonia became independent in 988 after the Franks declined to send support against the Moors.

FOR EIXAMPLE

In 1859, officials approved a plan for the Eixample, the grandiose extension of Barcelona beyond the city walls. The plan was developed in the late 19th and early 20th century, with many *modernista* buildings.

1131–62 Ramon Berenguer IV reigns and the union of Catalonia and Aragon takes place. Barcelona becomes a major trading city.

1213–76 Jaume I reigns, and conquers Valencia, Ibiza and Mallorca from the Moors. New city walls are built.

1354 The legislative council of Catalonia sets up the Generalitat to control city finances.

1410 Martí I, the last ruler of the House of Barcelona, dies without an heir. Catalonia is now ruled from Madrid.

1462–73 The Catalan civil war rages and the economy deteriorates.

1640 Els Segadors (the Reapers) revolt against Castilian rule.

1714 Barcelona defeated by French and Spanish troops in the War of the Spanish Succession. Catalonia made a Spanish province.

1813 Napoleonic troops depart. Textile manufacturing leads to a growth in the city's industry and population.

1888 The Universal Exhibition attracts 2 million visitors.

1909 Barcelona's churches and convents are set aflame during the Setmana Tràgica (Tragic Week).

PHILIP. V.

FARMACIA

1914–18 Barcelona's economy is boosted by Spanish neutrality in World War I.

1931 The Catalan Republic is declared after the exile of King Alfonso XIII.

1936–9 Spanish Civil War between Republicans and Franco's Nationalists, who win. Franco rules as dictator until his death. Spain remains neutral during World War II.

1975 Franco dies and the monarchy is restored. King Juan Carlos I allows the re-establishment of the Generalitat as the parliament of an autonomous regional government of Catalonia.

1992 Barcelona hosts the summer Olympic Games.

2004 Barcelona hosts the UNESCO Universal Forum of Cultures.

2007 The Spanish Government recognizes Catalonia as a "nation" in the constitution.

2009 Barcelona airport's new terminal opens with capacity for 55 million passengers per year.

2010 Pope Benedict XVI consecrates the Sagrada Família.

2017 Catalans vote for independence in an unauthorized referendum. Spanish government takes direct control of Catalan affairs.

FRANCO

In 1936, armed workers in Barcelona defeated an army uprising led by Nationalist General Franco. But resistance to Franco was weakened by internal strife between Communists and Anarchists. In 1939, Barcelona fell to the Nationalists. Catalan identity and culture were crushed during the subsequent Franco dictatorship. The Catalan language was banned and the region suffered economic decline. When Franco died in 1975, a constitutional monarchy was restored under which Catalonia regained its autonomy.

From left: A statue of St. George at the Generalitat; Felipe V of Spain; the Monument à Colom; an old Barcelonan street; modernista buildings in the Ramblas; General Franco

Index

Barcelona 25 Best

WRITTEN BY Michael Ivory
ADDITIONAL WRITING Sally Roy
UPDATED BY Mary-Ann Gallagher
SERIES EDITOR Clare Ashton
COVER DESIGN Chie Ushio, Yuko Inagaki
DESIGN WORK Tom Whitlock and Liz Baldin
IMAGE RETOUCHING AND REPRO Ian Little

Published in the United Kingdom by AA Publishing

ISBN 978-1-64097-090-8

EIGHTH EDITION

Color separation by AA Digital Department
Printed and bound by Leo Paper Products, China

10 9 8 7 6 5 4 3 2 1

A05593
Maps in this title produced from mapping © MAIRDUMONT / Falk Verlag 2016
Transport map © Communicarta Ltd, UK

The Automobile Association would like to thank the following photographers, companies and picture libraries for their assistance in the preparation of this book.

2 AA/M Jourdan; 3 AA/M Jourdan; 4t AA/M Jourdan; 4l AA/S Day; 5t AA/M Jourdan; 5 AA/S Day; 6t AA/M Jourdan; 6cl AA/M Jourdan; 6c AA/M Chaplow; 6cr AA/S Day; 6bl AA/M Chaplow; 6bc AA/M Chaplow; 6br AA/M Chaplow; 7t AA/M Jourdan; 7cl AA/S Day; 7c AA/S Day; 7cr AA/M Jourdan; 7bl AA/M Chaplow; 7bc AA/M Chaplow; 7br AA/S Day; 8t AA/M Jourdan; 9t AA/M Jourdan; 10t AA/M Jourdan; 10tr AA/S McBride; 10ctr AA/S McBride; 10cbr AA/S McBride; 10br AA/M Chaplow; 11t AA/M Jourdan; 11tl AA/S McBride; 11ctl AA/S McBride; 11cbl AA/S McBride; 11bl AA/S McBride; 12t AA/M Jourdan; 12bl AA/M Chaplow; 13t AA/M Jourdan; 13tl AA/M Jourdan; 13ctl AA/S McBride; 13cl Digital Vision; 13cbl Photodisc; 13bl Brand X Pics; 14t AA/M Jourdan; 14tr AA/S McBride; 14ctr AA/S McBride; 14cbr AA/S McBride; 14br AA/S McBride; 15t AA/M Jourdan; 15br AA/S McBride; 16t AA/M Jourdan; 16tr AA/S McBride; 16cr AA/S McBride; 16br AA/S Day; 17t AA/M Jourdan; 17tl AA/S Day; 17ctl AA/S Day; 17cbl AA/M Chaplow; 17bl AA/S McBride; 18t AA/M Jourdan; 18tr AA/S Day; 18ctr AA/M Chaplow; 18cbr AA/S Day; 18br AA/M Jourdan; 19t AA/S Day; 19ct AA/M Jourdan; 19c AA/M Jourdan; 19cb AA/M Jourdan; 19b AA/M Chaplow; 20/1 AA/M Chaplow; 24/5 AA/M Jourdan; 25tr AA/M Jourdan; 25cr AA/P Wilson; 26/7 AA/S Day, © 2011 Calder Foundation, New York / DACS London; 27 AA/P Wilson, © Succession Miro/ADAGP, Paris and DACS, London 2011; 28 AA/M Chaplow; 28/9 AA/M Jourdan; 30l AA/S Day; 30r AA/S Day; 31l AA/M Jourdan; 31c AA/M Jourdan; 31r AA/M Jourdan; 32t AA/S Day; 32b AA/M Jourdan; 33 AA/M Bonnet; 34t AA/S Day; 34bl AA/M Jourdan; 34br AA/P Wilson; 35t AA/C Sawyer; 36t AA/S McBride; 37t Digital Vision; 36c AA/M Jourdan; 38t AA/S McBride; 39 AA/S Day; 42l AA/S Day; 42/3t AA/S Day; 42/3c AA/S Day; 43tr AA/M Jourdan; 43cr AA/M Jourdan; 44 AA/M Jourdan; 44/5 AA/S Day; 46 AA/M Jourdan; 46/7t AA/M Chaplow; 46/7c AA/S Day; 47 AA/M Jourdan; 48l AA/M Bonnet; 48c AA/M Bonnet; 48r AA/S Day; 48l AA/S Day; 48c AA/P Wilson; 48r AA/M Chaplow; 49l AA/S McBride; 49r AA/S McBride; 50t AA/S Day; 50bl AA/P Wilson; 50br AA/P Wilson; 51t AA/S Day; 51b AA/S Day; 52 AA/S McBride; 53t AA/S McBride; 54t AA/M Chaplow; 55t Digital Vision; 56 AA/M Jourdan; 57t AA/S McBride; 58t AA/S McBride; 59 Ricard Pla and Pere Vivas/Palau de la Música Catalana; 62l AA/M Jourdan; 62r AA/M Jourdan; 63l AA/M Chaplow; 63c AA/M Chaplow; 63r Las Meninas, No. 30 (1957), Pablo Picasso, Pablo/Museu Picasso, Barcelona, Spain, Giraudon/The Bridgeman Art Library, © Succession Picasso/DACS, London 2011; 64l AA/M Jourdan; 64r Ricard Pla and Pere Vivas/Palau de la Música Catalana; 65l AA/M Chaplow; 65c AA/M Jourdan; 65r AA/M Jourdan; 66l AA/S Day; 66r AA/P Wilson; 67l AA/M Chaplow; 67r AA/M Chaplow; 68l AA/M Jourdan; 68/9t AA/S Day; 68cr AA/M Jourdan; 69cl AA/M Jourdan; 69r AA/M Jourdan; 70l AA/M Jourdan; 70/1 AA/P Wilson; 71 AA/S Day; 72t AA/S Day; 72bl AA/M Jourdan; 72br AA/M Jourdan; 73 AA/C Sawyer; 74t AA/S McBride; 75t AA/S McBride; 76t Photodisc; 77t AA/C Sawyer; 78t AA/S McBride; 78br AA/C Sawyer; 79 AA/S Day; 82 AA/S Day; 82/3 AA/S Day; 83t AA/M Chaplow; 83cl AA/S Day; 83cr AA/M Jourdan; 84 AA/M Bonnet; 85l AA/M Jourdan; 85r AA/M Chaplow; 86l AA/P Wilson; 86/7 AA/S Day; 86cr AA/S Day; 87r AA/M Jourdan; 87c AA/M Chaplow; 88 AA/S Day; 88/9t AA/M Jourdan; 88/9c AA/S Day; 89 AA/M Jourdan; 90 AA/S Day; 90/1 AA/M Jourdan; 91 AA/S Day; 92t AA/S Day; 92bl AA/M Jourdan; 92br AA/M Chaplow; 93t AA/C Sawyer; 93r AA/M Chaplow; 94t AA/M Chaplow; 95t AA/S McBride; 96t Digital Vision; 97t AA/S McBride; 98t AA/C Sawyer; 99 AA/S Day; 102/3t AA/M Jourdan; 102cl AA/M Jourdan; 102/3c AA/S Day; 103 AA/M Jourdan; 104l AA/M Bonnet; 104r AA/M Bonnet; 105t AA/S Day; 105b AA/M Bonnet; 106t AA/S Day; 106bl LH Images/Alamy; 106br AA/S Day; 107 AA/S McBride; 108t AA/C Sawyer; 108tr AA/S McBride; 108ctr AA/S McBride; 108cbr AA/C Sawyer; 108br AA/M Chaplow; 109t AA/C Sawyer; 110t AA/C Sawyer; 111t AA/C Sawyer; 112t AA/C Sawyer; 113 AA/S Day; 114t AA/S McBride; 115t AA/S McBride; 116t AA/S McBride; 117t AA/S McBride; 118t AA/S McBride; 119t AA/S McBride; 120t AA/S McBride; 120l AA/M Jourdan; 121t AA/S McBride; 122t AA/S McBride; 122t AA/M Chaplow; 122r AA/M Chaplow; 123t AA/S McBride; 124t AA/S McBride; 124bl AA/P Wilson; 124bc AA/AA; 124br AA/P Wilson; 124/5b AA/AA; 125t AA/S McBride; 125bc AA/M Jourdan; 125br Illustrated London News.

Every effort has been made to trace the copyright holders, and we apologise in advance for any unintentional omissions or errors. We would be pleased to apply any corrections in a following edition of this publication.

Titles in the Series

- Amsterdam
- Bangkok
- Barcelona
- Boston
- Brussels and Bruges
- Budapest
- Chicago
- Dubai
- Dublin
- Edinburgh
- Florence
- Hong Kong
- Istanbul
- Krakow
- Las Vegas
- Lisbon
- London
- Madrid
- Melbourne
- Milan
- Montréal
- Munich
- New York City
- Orlando
- Paris
- Rome
- San Francisco
- Seattle
- Shanghai
- Singapore
- Sydney
- Tokyo
- Toronto
- Venice
- Vienna
- Washington, D.C.